Back to Better

Annabelle Z Morris

With love and thanks to my family, past and present, dedicated to my family, present and future.

JANUARY 2021

5 January 2021

Blimey! Seventeen thousand, seven hundred and ninety-eight steps! The most I've walked since last September in the Lake District. Which strikes me that I spend a lot of my time comparing. Comparing to what I, or others, have or haven't done before. I'm not sure that's entirely healthy. I regularly read that achievers set goals. What about a goal just to survive for a bit? Isn't that still a goal?

Life seems to be driven by targets. We have them at work. And now our leisure time is full of targets too. Not that I see many people now. But who doesn't wear a fit-bit, or similar? Who isn't striving to lose weight, drink or smoke less, save more money, bake more, or spend more quality time with their children?

Maybe my 2021 target should be to steer clear of all targets. I do a great job and I keep a clean house. I'd like to think I'm thoughtful and kind. Why isn't that enough?

And there's another thing. I think that I think too much. My husband would say, I overthink. How is that even possible?

What's that radio show that has a thought for the day? Just one? Now I don't know how many thoughts I have. I have just googled* it. (* Other search engines are available). A few sites suggest I may have six thousand thoughts per day. Others suggest between sixty thousand and eighty thousand. Either way, it's a lot of thoughts. In fact, apart from breathing, it's probably what I do most of each day. And if I didn't think, that would probably be indicative that I am dead. Of course, that also holds true for breathing, or more accurately, for not breathing.

So, here's my thought for the day. I do loads of thinking. My supposedly decreasing brain capacity is full of thoughts. So, sod off with your thought for the day, that's supposed to make the listener feel better. I've got enough other stuff to remember without someone who probably wears socks and sandals forcing another one on me.

6 January 2021

I struggled to sleep last night. That's not unusual for many people right now. Except that I am currently on annual leave and can normally sleep on a washing line, for ten hours solid, no matter what time of the day or night, or my state of sobriety.

I just had so much going around my head (thus proving yesterday's observation that I don't need more thoughts for the day).

It seems my husband was also troubled. At one point he gave me an almighty bruise-inducing kick in my shin and declared, "The Indians are coming to get me." Typically, this happened just as I was about to nod off, thus delaying my slumber further.

I'm sure the main reason for my insomnia is my general state of being p'd off. I could easily list several contributory factors, including being repeatedly reminded I am one of the lucky ones in this pandemic mess in which we find ourselves. Why do I end up feeling guilty that I am annoyed?

I agree that there are many people far worse off than me. There always have been, and no doubt, always will be. That saddens me for them. But it doesn't change it or negate my own troubles. Let's face it, unless you're at the bottom of the luck-ladder, there is always someone else worse off.

How does it help to point that out to someone? Why isn't it balanced with the equally factual opposite truth that there's busloads of people better off than me (depending on how you define it, I suppose).

But assuming, (not unreasonably, in my opinion), that I am not number one on the luck-ladder, or even in the top one hundred thousand, there's loads of people better off than me. It is genuinely good news. I'm not jealous. I don't wish them any downturn. But they'll have troubles too, and being better off than others won't necessarily cure those troubles.

Look at Whitney Houston's tragic story. I watched *Can I be me?* the other day. Whether you liked her, or her music, or not, you surely couldn't deny she was blessed with a gifted voice. It would also seem she was weighed down by insecurities that led to drug addictions. She died aged forty-eight. Sorry if you didn't know that but I assumed a spoiler alert wasn't necessary. In around fifteen months, I shall be forty-eight, all being well, and honestly, the alternative doesn't bear thinking about.

I don't think about the alternative, much. It's not what's currently keeping me awake. I've tried my mindfulness techniques in vain over recent nights. They have helped me get to sleep before, but like regular painkiller users, maybe I have become desensitised to its effects. Maybe I'm just not sufficiently bought in to all this "being in the moment" stuff. How much more "in the moment" can I be, than lying in my own bed, next to my husband being chased by Indians, trying to get to sleep?

8 January 2021

2:27am! That's what time I woke up this morning with a bursting bladder. It's no wonder I feel permanently tired if I can't sleep through the night. This must be what parenthood feels like. We chose not to be parents, partly because we like sleep. (We also like being able to afford things and enjoy them not being made sticky by the inquisitive hands of toddlers). Given my bladder so regularly interrupts my sleep, I may as well just give it a name, as I would with a child. Billy. I shall name my bladder, Billy.

If I elected to have any surgery, it wouldn't be lip fillers, rhinoplasty, or liposuction. I would choose a larger Billy. I got out of the bath four times yesterday to pee! It's just not normal. Admittedly, I was in the bath for two hours, but still. Admittedly, I did drink nearly a bottle of wine while in the bath. But still.

I blame my best friend for the wine consumption, for sending me a new bath tray on which fits my glass and the bottle. To be fair, I don't really blame her. I try not to live in a blame culture. Events here in the UK since our first lockdown last March, serve as a reminder to me of what a lack of personal responsibility can do. It spreads disease. That could be a metaphor, but in 2020/2021, it's sadly true.

Anyway, it still can't be usual to want to pee as soon as you lie down in a bath. It's as if I suffer with involuntary osmosis, sucking up the bath water while I wallow, which I then need to promptly expel.

Regardless, I enjoyed that long bath, partly thanks to my new bath tray. When I sent my best friend a photo of it in place, she was amused I had a whole bottle of wine on it, and not just a glass. I did suggest that she and I could fall out, and that it was our philanthropic, civil duty to help replenish Rishi Sunak's tax coffers that are two trillion in debt and growing. As a business advisor, I know that's not good news! A glass of wine isn't going to cut it.

9 January 2021

My head hurts. Of course, it's entirely my own fault. Having been largely, and very exceptionally, dry, over Christmas and New Year due to illness, it seems my husband and I embarked on a mission to catch up in one single night. We drank far too much from the wine fridge we had installed two years ago when we had the kitchen and dining room renovated. I should learn that it isn't our sole responsibility to refill the tax coffers. Nevertheless, we gave it a good go.

I originally woke this morning with a smug and premature sense of security, without a headache. My husband brought me a cup of tea in bed and ibuprofen. I foolishly declined the ibuprofen.

It's simply the loveliest thing my husband does for me every day. Well, make me tea to drink in bed is. He doesn't always feel the need to accompany it with ibuprofen. We're not alcoholics. Apparently, alcoholism is an unusual drinking pattern. How can a pattern be unusual? And what's unusual for a childless adult stuck at home on a Friday night? Why do I keep asking myself questions to which I don't know the answer?

Anyway, for whatever reason, I can barely function without a morning cup of tea. If I'm entirely honest, there's also the distinct possibility that it gives me a seemingly valid excuse to procrastinate getting out of bed and functioning.

"Just finishing my tea, babe," I'll retort if asked when I'm getting up. I don't have a throat of asbestos. That's reserved for parents, who seem to have to consume everything immediately and at lightning speed, or they may not get chance to finish it otherwise, and so need a fireproof oesophagus. I, however, cannot consume anything so quickly, and instead can drag out tea drinking for a good forty-five minutes. That must be reserved for childless people. I can't imagine anyone who has time for forty-five-minute cups of tea in bed, must also selflessly care for another human being sufficiently well to keep it alive.

James Martin on television gave us another two hours to procrastinate functioning. Unfortunately, that gave my hangover chance to unexpectedly hit me like an Eddie Stobart truck. Where are those pills?

Our subsequent daily walk around the village cured my thick head. My husband cursed several drivers without their fog lights on. I suggested that those with automatic light settings may not realise they need to manually switch on their fog lights. He suggested I gave them all too much credit and they are just stupid, selfish pricks.

Maybe I am deliberately and desperately trying to find some credit to give. I certainly applaud anyone right now for just keeping going. I thought I was tough. I've never needed three weeks off work in almost twenty working years; my own mini circuit-break. How did I get so exhausted without children? How did I get so sad and so consumed by the grief of losing friends during lockdown? It doesn't matter really. What matters, is that I keep going. Is it too early for more wine?

10 January 2021

My head hurts, again! Which I expected, to be fair. Last night was quite probably the best night in with clothes on of the last ten months.

Our very good friends bought the game *Outsmarted*. It's like *Trivial Pursuit* crossed with *Who Wants to be a Millionaire*. After a few false starts when I was concerned that we may be left playing *I Spy*, it worked brilliantly. Which is just as well, because playing *I Spy* remotely from three different households on a group messenger call, surely wouldn't have worked. It was slightly embarrassing while simultaneously very pleasing that Hubby and I won all four *Outsmarted* games!

Of course, we consumed a fair few beverages over the seven hours. Our recycling bin can't cope, and I refuse to put the empties in the black bin. Anyway, I can't do that even if I was minded to, because we couldn't be bothered to put it out last week, and so the black bin is rammed.

Couldn't be bothered! Not because we're jealous that the bin goes out more than we do, although that is true. We just couldn't be bothered which shames me. There were people in America last week, so incensed that they stormed the Capitol Building. I don't condone that. I genuinely don't understand how rioting, supposedly in the name of democracy, achieves anything other than irony, given I thought democracy should afford the right to live in peace. But we couldn't even be bothered to put the bin out, let alone demonstrate.

15:50.

I'm dressed! I will succeed in convincing myself that is a worthy achievement.

Of course, being dressed means I've thrown on a big sloppy jumper and my Christmas gift pyjama bottoms over my underwear, as with every other day for the last two hundred or so.

If I am honest, I may not even have bothered doing that if I was flat chested. No one my size should have to fight gravity while braless, ever! I recall Marilyn Monroe once said women should only wear a smile and perfume in bed. Well, I could put forward a very strong argument in favour of adding a bra to that shortlist. I woke up the other day and thought my boobs had been stolen in the night, until I found them under my armpits.

Armpits, incidentally, would be my evidence in support of us having been created, rather than the widely accepted view that we evolved. There must be a chance that the same person that invented deodorant, invented human beings. Only a human would be so sufficiently sophisticated to be able to keep warm by trapping air amongst body hair, and cool itself down by sweating, but then insist on spending fortunes in money and time defuzzing and buying deodorant. Why do we ignore what was so ingeniously designed? It sounds like a money spinner for a deodorant manufacturer to me.

Speaking of which, there's also all the money we spend on other beauty products. Victoria Wood, one of the best observational comedians ever, once described lipstick as "overpriced bits of grease." That superb description could arguably apply to various other beauty-related products, and I have my fair share of them. Many are from the beautiful advent calendar from Liberty that my husband bought me. The trouble is, by the time I have smeared broccoli and poppy-seed serum* on my face; whale semen eye gel* on my lids; Tefal line-reducing cream* round my mouth; dodo urine* on my cuticles; and Brazilian bum-bum cream on my neck and cleavage, I've spent fifteen minutes trying to look younger than I was when I started, and have only succeeded in being fifteen minutes older.

* Not real products to my knowledge, but you get the gist. The only one that is real, the Brazilian bum-bum cream, sounds

like I'll end up with even more bum than before, and now it's going to be on my neck and cleavage. Maybe I should stop slavering myself in goo. I'd save lots of time and I'd have more money for wine. And I'm sure wine paralyses more muscles anyway, so drinking it instead of buying beauty products, is probably more effective as an anti-ageing strategy.

11 January 2021

2:27am. Again! And 4:32. And 6:12. And 6:30 when the alarm went off. My husband says needing to pee so frequently is in my head. It's not. It's in Billy, and then promptly in the toilet. Admittedly, I don't compete with a racehorse, but as a non-golden shower household, Hubby should be glad I visit the en suite each time.

It's my first day back at work since 9 December. I have around three hundred emails. At least I won't also be distracted by posts on Linked-In and Twitter, as I have deleted both apps from my phone. I did the same with the Facebook app last August, initially for a one-month experiment. By around the end of September, three people had got in touch with me asking how I was, as they hadn't seen any of my posts for well over a month. Three people! One. Two. Three. The same number of times I got up in the night.

Conversely, it felt like I read thousands of negative posts. I read posts that were just ranting about the state of affairs; blaming others for said state without accepting any personal responsibility at all, or otherwise back-stabbing people unknown to the critic. Occasionally there was a hilarious video of some pet antics, or someone's Sunday lunch. But overall, I realised that bombarding my brain continually with other people's negativity was contributing to my own downward mood spiral.

I'd really known this for much longer. I have no idea why I hadn't previously deleted the app. Chris Evans hasn't even had a mobile phone for two years and he seems happier than a dog licking himself. It's like he falls out of a bucket of excrement each morning into a barrel of boobs. He's that happy. I too, am more positive without Facebook.

To be fair, there's some relevant and helpful work-related posts on Linked-In and Twitter. Although I'd like to believe if the information is that crucial, I'd read about it in one of the various technical bulletins or other updates I receive from numerous third parties. Even without social media apps, I have enough repositories to read. (I always mix up the word repository with suppository, which could pose problems, and isn't an error I should ever make more than once).

Those repositories of information include Microsoft Teams channels to check for updates, as well as the aforementioned apps that I have heard some people call Stalk-book; let's link up and Tw*tter. Oh, and I also have a work landline and mobile phone, which normally ring simultaneously with people asking questions that need answering.

I feel like a Royal Mail depot at Covid Christmas, except I don't have any little vans transporting the various queries to someone else to open and deal with. They're incessant. Every day. Every week. The queries don't stop because I am tired, or because I am grieving. I kept receiving emails while I was absent. My out of office message between 9 December and 4 January 2021 automatically responded saying I was ill. Yet I have also had chasing emails or messages from people in the same period, asking why I haven't replied to the earlier query. I apologised that the automated notice of my illness must not have worked. Apparently it did work, but some of the recipients of it assumed I'd email back from a portable device.

Maybe I can secure my retirement and escape the emails, by making a fortune disproving a well-established theory. Of course, I am not smart enough to disprove anything like evolution. Not least, because I think evolution is true. I don't really think we were created by Mr Sure. (Other deodorants are available). I'd need the brain the size of Stephen Hawking or Stephen Fry to be sufficiently convincing in any argument against a widely accepted doctrine.

I'm sure there are people with other forenames than Stephen, who could disprove something. Like Brian May, perhaps. The other night, I was sitting in what is now our Queen Corner of the kitchen. The mini Red Special guitar I bought my husband for Christmas hangs on a wall along with Queen first-day issue stamps and other memorabilia. As I was sitting there, I said it felt most unfair that not only was Brian May an exceptionally talented musician, but he could also hold court amongst NASA members, and has an asteroid named after him.

Which is why evolution must be true. If we'd been created, surely a right-minded inventor would have spread the talent around a bit more. May's also an animal rights' activist with a head of hair that his own wife could envy, despite her own very full mane, and he's never gained weight! It's impossible not to be impressed by him, or feel slightly inadequate.

While May will leave behind a legacy of music adored by millions and an eponymous asteroid, I won't even leave a Teddy Bear named after me, and I named my own Teddy Bears.
But even plankton serve a purpose. And we all need to be kinder about our own achievements.

My mum, bless her, insists on writing all my designations after my name when written on envelopes. The postman must wonder who handwrites to me in this way, especially when the nineteen letters don't fit. Unperturbed, Mum turns the envelope over to accommodate the overflow.

The last five letters are awarded to anyone who pays an annual subscription to my profession's trade body. That still leaves fourteen letters, which represent four years studying for a Law with French degree, and another four years studying in evenings after full-time work, to become a business advisor. Yet despite all my academic achievements, one of my strongest educational memories is being asked as an eight-year-old, what happened to the two percent I didn't get in a maths exam.

I got ninety-eight percent and was made to feel like a failure. Or at least, I reacted to the question as if I was a failure. I now know that others don't have some super-power to make me feel one way or another. It's just how I reacted at the time. I could have chosen to react differently. But thirty-nine years ago, I hadn't got almost forty-seven years of life experience, so I didn't know any better.

I still remember that three students got one hundred percent. I have never forgotten that I didn't also achieve perfection. The teacher told us to write four pound signs at the start of the answers to a four-part question halfway through the paper. She told us we'd forget by the time we got to that question, and each pound sign was worth one half of a mark. I was foolishly overly confident in my own memory. I forgot to write those pounds signs, and thirty-nine years later I still haven't forgiven myself.

I tell work colleagues that perfection isn't necessary. I tell them that eighty percent is usually good enough. I tell them the law of diminishing returns means that spending more time for that extra twenty percent isn't merited or proportionate.

And there's instances where significantly less than eighty percent suffices. I'm perfectly happy with thirteen percent for a bottle of white or red, for example. At the end of the first year of my four-year degree, forty percent was enough to proceed to the second year. Admittedly from then on, it was wise to aim higher and I was thrilled with a respectable Desmond 2:2, only a couple of percent off a 2:1.

I spent my third year of that degree at Strasbourg University, studying French law. In French! (Bien sûr). Well that surely must count as an achievement. Apparently, the UK's average adult reading age is nine years old, and I studied law, in French. We all have achievements. Whether we bring up a child; grow something; make someone laugh in their darkest moments; or manage to get dressed before 10am, 11am, noon at the weekend, we should remember our achievements. We should be kinder to ourselves and to others, especially today and for the foreseeable future when so many are having to home-school again. I usually resist making any suggestions about parenthood. I resist as other parents claim I couldn't possibly understand what it's like, even though I was a child for many years of my life which clearly left some deep-rooted memories.

If I dared to comment, I'd like to ask every parent to be kind to themselves and to their children. I'd also ask parents to count to ten the next time they want to castigate a teacher. Teachers cope with around thirty children at a time. None of the children are the teacher's own. Children can be like bodily smells. Those from your own household are just about bearable, but anyone else's may take your breath away, and not in a good way.

So, I'd like to ask parents to be kind to our teachers please. My sister is one and she is awesome. I'd like to ask parents to be kind to their children. They are our future. But I'd better keep my mouth shut, as I can't possibly understand how difficult parenthood is.

I'll stick with trying to be kind to myself and hope it rubs off.

17:30

I'm not watching today's government briefing, given by Matt Hancock, Health Secretary. The news app on my phone told me the dreaded stats. There have been five hundred and twenty-nine more deaths and forty-six thousand, one hundred and sixty-nine cases. We never thought ten months ago we would be in lockdown now. I've not been with my parents, my sister, and her family, for a year. My parents don't have the internet or smart phones to be able to video call. But as tempting as visiting may be, we are staying focussed on keeping us all safe.

Mr M and I stayed in last year from 16 March, a week before the enforced lockdown. We're not going out. We're certainly not going out-out. If you haven't seen Micky Flanagan's sketch about going out-out, it will make sense once you have. And it might just have you roaring with tear-inducing laughter as it does with us, every time we watch it.

We're thankful for wine deliveries and that dry January was abolished. It wasn't abolished! Really?

12 January 2021

I slept right through, which is just as well, as we're down to the toilet rolls on the holders. I hadn't appreciated how much of the stuff we get through. Of course, it's increased since we've both been permanently working from home.

And wfh is great for me. In each of the recent few years, I averaged over one hundred nights away in hotels while working. Now that adds up to a lot of hotel points, I can't currently spend. It must also have represented a huge saving on our shopping bill given how much toilet roll I now realise we use.

Of course, my overactive bladder doesn't help. Overactive almost sounds like an achievement, doesn't it? It isn't. Billy struggles as soon as I lie down and so just acts like a tea strainer. Maybe I shouldn't have thrown away that fifty pence voucher for Tena lady, but Mr M has put the bin out, so there's no retrieving it now.

Of course, it shouldn't worry me that we're down to six rolls, as we have an order for more included in the supermarket delivery coming tomorrow. Some might suggest we're lucky to have toilet roll. It's hardly a benchmark for luck in the western world is it? We don't even use quilted, so that thought about being lucky can just bog off.

These renewed lockdown days are squeaky bum times though. It's less than a year ago in March 2020 that the shelves were bare as people panic-bought toilet rolls during that lockdown.

People also panic-bought tinned tomatoes, as if toilet roll and tinned tomatoes are a natural two-some. They're not. If people had panic-bought Leicestershire and Birmingham's combined supply of curry, and bought thirty-six packs of toilet roll, I could understand. But tinned tomatoes and loo roll go together like jogging pants and stilettoes. Nothing says I'm not really a fitness fanatic like wearing stilettoes with clothes that should only be seen on a fitness fanatic.

That fashion combo looks as ridiculous as seeing heels grace the Welford Road terraces, where Leicester Tigers' fans stand to watch the rugby (union). Don't get me wrong. I love a good four and a half inches. I love my Choos so much, I had a shoe cabinet handmade for them. But there's a time and a place. And neither with jogging pants, nor at the Tigers' is the time for stilettoes. Mind you, I'd donate our last toilet roll in return for being able to stand on those terraces this weekend laughing at the inappropriate fashions.

The panic-buying scenes in March 2020 were truly abhorrent to me. Only one month earlier, after Caroline Flack sadly took her own life on 15 February 2020, people across the country called en masse for kindness to all.

And here we were watching video footage on the news of elderly men and women carrying empty shopping baskets staring at empty shelves. Some of those shoppers when interviewed, said they couldn't afford to bulk buy and stock up, and so the empty shelves posed real problems to them.

Some customers literally fought off pensioners for the last pasta packet. The selfishness was chilling. My paternal grandad volunteered to serve in the RAF's Bomber Command in WW11. Like so many others, he gave his life for our country, shot down in the fateful Nuremberg raid on 31 March 1944. He was twenty-six years old. His son, my dad, was only two. Conversely, last March, some of our population my grandad gave his life for, wouldn't dream of letting a war veteran have the last bag of carbs.

Thankfully, we did also hear lots of heart-warming stories of kindness and selfless acts. We were personally overwhelmed by the outpouring from local villagers when we appealed for unwanted vegetables so I could make soup for any in need.

When I look, there are acts of kindness everywhere. I just need to avoid anyone that looks like they may stick their stiletto in my forehead, like a scene from *Single White Female*, just to get the last bag of risotto rice.

18:15

Time to make dinner, and we'd better have some risotto rice.

Risotto is my meal of choice most Tuesdays and Thursdays. Mr M doesn't join me eating it. He does that Jacqueline Whiteheart 5:2 plan that means he only consumes eight hundred calories on those days. I probably imbibe that in white coffee by noon.

To be fair to Jacqueline's recipes, I have eaten the chicken, tomato, and pasta dish that Hubby has for his dinner. It's delicious, and I feel full after it. That satisfaction may be due, at least in part, to eating what I call a proper breakfast and lunch, compared to Mr M's oxygen and water servings. So, I tend not to eat the same as him on Tuesdays or Thursdays. Also, it's only fair to the panic-buyers that we don't consume more than our fair share of pasta and tinned tomatoes, so I cook for myself.

Risotto gives me an excuse (not needed) to open wine, as it's in the recipe, which means I can also legitimately pour myself a glass or two. I always feel slightly guilty that I am savouring some of the finest Sauvignon Blanc that New Zealand has to offer, while Mr M increases his body's water content to about eighty percent.

It's ironic that the acronym of my favourite wine is SB, as that's my nickname for Mr M. The acronym doesn't represent wine in that case, but may explain why I think about it so much.

I sometimes cook ~~the risotto~~ without wine. Let's be honest, I'd finish the bottle otherwise, and that would be my eight hundred calories.

Who are these people that open a bottle of white, and have leftovers in the fridge for days? Or that make some wine ice cubes for the freezer for future use to keep white wine cold without diluting it? Just drink it more quickly. Problem solved. People can be so defeatist.

Besides, it's winter and we can't venture further than the

end of our increasing lockdown stomachs, let alone go anywhere that showers vitamin D and warmth on anything. We don't need wine ice cubes taking room in the freezer.

Anyway, as I continue to try to drink less, risotto without wine it is. I've also noticed that if I wear my fit-bit on my stirring hand, I can clock up a few miles without even running anywhere.

I don't jog on the spot while stirring, in a multitasking whirlwind that should only be attempted by drivers who repeatedly clench and release their bottom cheeks while sitting at red lights as part of their daily exercise regime. I really don't understand why they don't just run to where they are going if they are that desperate for a work-out.

I just stir, for about forty minutes. To me, it's cathartic and peaceful. Others may think it's about forty minutes of their life they won't get back. Which may be true, although I did simultaneously watch House of Games, and I learnt something.

Brian May has designed a sport bra. It's true. I checked. I would have believed it more easily if Meatloaf was the protagonist of the story. Meatloaf seems better equipped to help him achieve the best design.

As it is, Mr May's guitar business (BMG), and not Meatloaf, is selling five different sizes, all adorned with guitars. According to the website, the bras salute the guitar business, using the BMG colours, because "It doesn't have to be red to be special."

So now, I am stirring risotto, staring at the mini Red Special on our wall in Queen Corner, and a massive pair of 32FFs keep leaping out at me. Queen Corner is now Tit Corner.

I may just be guilty of treason by renaming Queen Corner in this way! Thankfully this country abolished the death penalty for treason in 1998.

Damn you though, Brian May. I may buy one of your bras, just so that there may be some semblance of truth when I say that you, your eponymous asteroid, your many talents, and your bras, are getting right on my tits now.

13 January 2021

Crikey. The USA has executed Lisa Montgomery by lethal injection. She was the killer in 2004 of an expectant mother. She took the unborn child by crude caesarean, to pass off as her own, and is the first woman to be executed on death row since 1953.

Her lawyer said execution was far from justice. There'll be many who agree with that view, although I don't understand how sixteen years of appeals and stays can serve proper justice either.

It sounds like her lawyers were hoping for another stay until after Joe Biden takes office. Mr Trump resumed federal executions after seventeen years without one. Ms Montgomery was the eleventh person since July 2020 to receive lethal injection in the jail in Indiana.

I've not read everything about the case. I certainly don't know how the American judicial system works, so I'm not sure what another stay may have achieved other than to postpone the execution further. Did she ever have a chance of release? I wasn't an expert at English or French law after studying them for four years, so I'm certainly not going to grasp the USA's system by reading a Wikipedia page.

Contrary to those that oppose the death penalty, there'll no doubt be many that receive news of the execution positively. Of course, the UK no longer has capital punishment for any crime. We live very freely compared to some other countries. Some countries would chop off your hand for stealing. How desperate must someone be to steal, knowing they may lose their hand? I'm grateful to live in a country where people don't have a hand taken off them for a criminal act that suggests they need just that, a helping hand.

14 January 2021

I wore my knickers back to front all day!

15 January 2021

Mr M's already made me tea, as always, and started the ironing. He's decided not to do any of his paid work, as he would ordinarily be on the golf course today anyway. He usually plays golf on Monday and Friday each week.

He's got various household chores he wants to get done, including making a stew for dinner in the slow cooker. I've asked him to load the stew with bay leaves, as we have the European Union's mountain of them. Which is ironic since we've left the EU.

It makes me laugh. Not leaving the EU itself. There's nothing about the last four and a half years that has been funny in my opinion. After four and a half years, we seem to have ended up with less fish than we hoped for, musicians may find touring more difficult, and the Erasmus scheme which allowed me to study in France all those years ago isn't available to UK students anymore. I'm so grateful I studied when it was. We may even end up needing visas or having to pay to go to EU countries on holiday.

Freedom of movement we had. Freedom of trade we had. Extra expense we shall now have. I'm sure there will also be advantages to leaving the EU, and we need to benefit from those opportunities.

What does make me laugh though, is the amount of people who used to ask me if we wouldn't be in Europe anymore. Not in Europe? Do they think the fifty-two percent that voted leave, have been paddling since June 2016, so that when we woke up on 1 January 2021, we'd have crossed that great big pond that is the Atlantic Ocean and become part of the Americas? Or perhaps that the rowers may have taken a different route, turned left at Cornwall, and ended up round the Cape of Good Hope at the bottom tip of South Africa until we became part of Australasia?

No! We will still be in Europe. It's the Union we've left.

Maybe those people thought that the vote was so influential, the catatonic plates would spontaneously shift until the UK became part of a different continent altogether.

I digress. I was curious however when I was putting this week's shopping away, why we'd ordered more bay leaves when we already had plenty, and use about one per year. My curiosity was satisfied last night when I was about to pour myself a Baileys. It seems that when I'd asked Alexa to add Baileys to the shopping list, she'd misheard and noted bay leaves instead. When Mr M printed the shopping list and submitted the online order, he not unreasonably assumed we needed bay leaves.

Now, I'm grateful that I can ask Alexa to add items to the shopping list without stopping whatever it is I am doing. I'm grateful that Mr M does the order, and it did make us both laugh when we realised the error. They say laughter is nature's own medicine. We should all laugh if we can, every day, as many times as we can. But I can't deny I'd have been even happier if I'd got some Baileys to drink!

Since Mr M has already decided what he'll do today, I won't tell him it's three and a half weeks since we washed the sheets. I know it is almost a month because I diarised when I last did it. It became necessary to diarise it, so that I can prove it to Hubby. He clearly never thought the weeks would fly by so quickly right now, and will often claim the sheets were only washed the other day.

I wonder though if SB just tries to convince us it's not been that long since we washed the sheets, so that he doesn't have to iron the bedding again. He does all the ironing in our house. I don't iron. I'm double crap at ironing. I would win gold if the competition was to be the worst at ironing. I used to buy things that stretched or were dry clean only. The latter got expensive and I've found that if I eat enough of Hubby's homemade cookies, I must stretch my clothes anyway. Well done, me. One less job to do, and I continue to avoid ironing for which I am truly thankful, particularly when it comes to bedding.

Let's face it, ironing sheets is the hard bit. Washing them

isn't difficult. I know you remove the bedding by hand. You load the machine, by hand. You take it from the machine, by hand, and put it in the tumble dryer, by hand. But it's not that hard. It's not like using a twin tub like my mum used to. That is hard work.

Ironing it all is also hard work. Not least as the board that is purposefully made so you can iron stuff, can't even properly accommodate anything other than pillowcases, without the item dragging on the floor, or becoming creased again when you try to iron the next part.

Who irons stretched, fitted sheets apart from my mother anyway, who claims that my dad feels creases otherwise? He should play the part of the Princess, in the Princess and the Pea for goodness' sake if that's true. If our fitted sheet is anything to go by, once it's stretched over the bed, like certain celebrities' skin over their faces, it doesn't need ironing.

Mr M and I have been married almost three and a half years. Is one week per year of marriage, before washing the bedsheets, an acceptable level of hygiene? I think I'd better just wash them this weekend. We won't even need to iron them anyway, as it's winter and we just chuck the matching throw over the top and hide any duvet cover creases.

The hardest part will be putting the cover back on the huge duvet. There's a common consensus that the easiest way to do it, is to turn the cover inside out, shove your hands inside it and grab the furthest corners. Then simultaneously, while your hands are in the cover holding the corners of it, grab the two duvet corners nearest to you, pull the duvet towards you, and just shake the cover over the rest of it.

Except it's not that simple. At 5'6" tall with a proportionate fingertip to tip span, I'm not sufficiently sized. I end up looking like a rabid pterodactyl with all the flapping and wafting, and shaking, and frothing at the mouth. Ironically, if I had the span of a pterodactyl, I wouldn't need to flap and froth.

For all that effort, the cover ends up no more than six inches over the rest of the duvet. That necessitates me walking round the bed and otherwise trying to pull the cover down over the rest of the duvet. It's impossible to do without the previously rooted duvet corners, working away from the other end of the cover.

I end up with about eight inches of duvet cover at the end it all began with no duvet content at all. The sides of the duvet always fold over themselves too, so there's great big bulges in the middle, bordered by nothing but unfilled duvet cover to keep my left arm warm. I despair.

I did have a brain wave earlier though when I was refilling the coffee bean hopper. The already open bag of coffee has a big bulldog clip on it to keep the bag tightly sealed and the beans fresh. How about if I put bulldog clips on the duvet corners before trying to pull the cover over the rest?

16 January 2021

Week one back at work successfully completed. I am fully dressed before 13:30. Not bad. I have removed the pre-Christmas, pre-lurgy remnants of nail varnish. The bed sheets are already washed and in the dryer. The aprons and other random items that often escape the wash-load are now in the machine, waiting for me to get the rest of the dark washing from the laundry basket upstairs. I am winning!

14:27

Why have I come upstairs?

17 January 2021

I've just put an empty egg box in the utility room, along with various others waiting for a good home with someone who can refill them. The washing machine door is open with aprons inside. That's why I went upstairs yesterday afternoon. To get the laundry. My brain is as much like a tea strainer as Billy is. I would normally chastise myself for being forgetful. Well, instead of being so self-critical, I've just gone and got the dirty clothes and switched on the machine.

What difference will one more day make? I have far too many clothes anyway. Or rather, I have too many clothes I don't wear. Yesterday, I donned clean clothes that had only just been ironed, much to Mr M's annoyance. Perhaps I should put an embargo on washing clothes and see just how many of the items in my wardrobes I wear.

12:40

I just spoke to my folks and had a good giggle. I always end up buoyed after speaking to them. Of course, I'd love to be able to be with my family again. I wrote in the Christmas card I sent them, that instead of being sad we can't hug and kiss, I was trying to be thankful that we have each other to miss.

The pool of other people that also love their parents seems to be much smaller than I assumed as a child. So, I'm grateful to feel loved by my parents. I'd previously have said I was lucky. I am certain that I am lucky, not least as being lucky, to me, suggests I had no influence over whatever has happened. I had nothing to do with anything about my birth. If anything, my sister had more influence, as I was a celebratory bonk on her first birthday.

Anyway, instead of just repeating how lucky I am, I am learning that being grateful for what I have, helps me to maintain a positive frame of mind. I listened to a webinar at work last week about resilience building. Of the various tools that assist building resilience, being grateful is one. The webinar host suggested people keep a gratitude book, noting down things for which we're thankful. I was given a gratitude book as a gift in 2019 and have filled a few pages, and it does help improve my mood as I write in it.

That said, it's quite difficult to express just how grateful I am for everything my parents did and do for me. They're my heroes. No doubt, with hindsight, they'd consider different parenting techniques for some situations. I'd make changes to my childhood behaviour too. I would certainly erase one time I'm embarrassed to recall. When I was twelve years old, my mum had taken my sister and me shopping. I demanded Mum bought me a second top, in addition to the one I had already chosen. Mum spent the last three pounds in her purse on me, forfeiting a treat for herself. I only wore that top once.

I also wouldn't have shied away from the hugs and kisses she tried to shower me with at the school gates, or when I came home from uni for the holidays. I can't change those times, but I can be a more selfless daughter now.

I can also think how I am around other people. It helps me if I surround myself with people that radiate warmth, which was another resilience-building tool mentioned on the webinar. While my positive mood is mine, I will happily share it. If I help people feel better, like propagating plants from cuttings, my positive mood also grows. Win, win. I just can't share any positivity if people doing impressions of positivity vacuums have sapped it all from me.

That's why I'm looking forward so much to talking with friends who live in South Africa later. We always have a laugh. There's an alcohol sale prohibition over there now, but their wine store is well stocked. Nevertheless, I'm appreciative to live here right now, despite the better SA climate. Did I take my Vitamin D tablet earlier?

19 January 2021

My dad's seventy-ninth birthday. I'll ring him after today's training course. As usual on our internal conferences, there's some well-being sessions from which I always learn at least one useful tip.

Apparently, being creative can help our mood and resilience. My sister-in-law says it helps her when she knits or crochets. She's generously given me various pieces, including my Wigan Warriors Rugby League lamb in cherry and white colours, my Tigers terrapin in the famous, red, green, and white colours, and my similarly branded scarf and hat which I (used to) wear to the Tigers' matches.

Conversely, I feel about as creative as a toilet duck. Unless someone points me in the right direction, and controls the manoeuvres, I produce something resembling frankly what could benefit from a bit of toilet duck. That said, I can colour in the lines of a painting more accurately than Picasso, and his paintings sell for millions.

I just struggle with invention or creation. I remember going to the cinema years ago to watch Tolkien's *Lord of the Rings (LOTR)*. I asked my mate early on what the heck one of the characters, Gollup (?), was meant to be. My mate promptly said I wouldn't enjoy the film, so I benefitted from a three-hour sleep instead. It was worth every penny.

I've tried to watch *LOTR* again, largely because so many people keep telling me how brilliant it is and how I absolutely must watch the entire film and series, read all the books, and buy the duvet cover. I've tried to watch more than once, at different times of the day or evening, and I always end up asleep. I just don't get along with the fantasy genre. I've never got on with Terry Pratchett's books, especially counting to three and then starting again but preceding numbers with many. One, two, three, many, many-one, many-two, many-three. When I went to school, we counted one, two, three, four, five, six, seven, eight. If our reading age averages nine, I'll bet our arithmetic age is about four, judging by Pratchett's popularity. I don't always react well when people insist I try again or am somehow stupid not to enjoy such literary marvels. It's just not my thing. It can't and doesn't make me stupid.

I find some judicial commentary interesting, often ingenious, and sometimes funny. But I don't insist that everyone goes away and reads the All England Law Reports. I don't read the important judgment of Bolton v Stone of 1951 to my mates who enjoy cricket. The House of Lords held a cricket club wasn't in breach of its duty. A player had hit a ball so high and far that it entered a neighbour's home, hitting and injuring Ms Stone. Lord

Denning said, "To my mind, [cricket] is a most reasonable use… For over seventy years [it] has been played on this ground to the great benefit of the community as a whole, and the injury of none."

I'm not belittling Ms Stone's injury, from which I understand she fully recovered, but well done Lord Denning. That deserves a clapping emoji if you ask me. Of course, the increasing use of abbreviations and emojis could be one reason for our population's decreasing literacy. I've only got to read the stats to know that many in this country are more likely to get the clap, than be able to spell it correctly.

Anyway, if I don't at least understand the concept behind a story, it's likely to induce a deep slumber, and so I tend to avoid anything fantasy related. I can sometimes enjoy stories of witches because I understand the concept. No doubt being a direct descendant of a Pendle witch helps to nurture my interest. I even had a witch tattooed on my back as homage to my ancestry. I remember on holiday once, when a French couple had obviously seen my tattoo and passed various comments about my sourcière. They both looked like they feared I may cast a spell on them when they realised I had understood every word. I was trying not to laugh out loud so they weren't further embarrassed at their incorrect assumption I wouldn't understand their language. It was almost as hilarious as being asked once if I could cast spells. I can cast spells about as well as I can paddle our island across the Atlantic.

20 January 2021

I really want to see my family in person.

22 January 2021

It feels like it's the first time in over four years that our news this week so far, hasn't been entirely consumed by Brexshit or Covid. Mr Trump's left the White House like a four-year-old leaving the chocolate factory. He's only the tenth president not to serve a second term, and the first since the early 1990s. Of course, he's claiming it's not his fault. According to Mr Trump, the voting system that brought him the presidency in the first place, was rigged. Perhaps he needs to focus more on why he didn't get such an overwhelming number of votes, that any (unproven) rigging wouldn't have made a difference.

In other unpublicised news, my dad had his first vaccine. Of course, it's been widely announced that those over seventy-five are receiving them. I am astounded at the pace at which we've secured these vaccines and are rolling them out. That's the news I want to hear. I want to hear and read positivity. Since March last year, the media seems to have been on a one-way journey to destroy our nation's community spirit and our faith that we would beat this virus together. Our population included so many that wanted to help others less fortunate, and was determined to commit to the common goal, whatever it took.

Yet our media bombarded our brains with subtle, and sometimes not so subtle concerns that different decisions should have been taken. Journalists asked confrontational and leading questions.

"Prime Minister, what if...? Why didn't you....? Shouldn't you have...? Isn't it true that...?"

The media even planted ideas in people's heads that weren't beneficial.

"What would you say, Professor Vallance, if someone was packing their cases tonight, to go to see family miles away before tomorrow's lockdown rules will prevent it?"

The Professor, not unexpectedly, said people should unpack their cases. Sadly, many wouldn't have heard him, as they would already have been up in the loft taking their cases down to pack and travel to the other side of the country, risking accidents that would further pressurise our hospitals, and making unnecessary contact with people.

How has any of that media coverage helped? What about if we asked the media, "Isn't it true to say that more of us may have adhered to the rules, and we may therefore have been in a better place now, if you hadn't planted irresponsible ideas in our minds? Wouldn't we have stuck to the guidance and law for longer, and in greater numbers, if you hadn't suggested the government constantly made the wrong decisions? What are your scientific qualifications that make your opinions wiser than those of our learned Professors?"

It all reminds me of a team building exercise at work once where each individual team was tasked at directing a blindfolded teammate around obstacles to get to the finishing line. The winning team celebrated. Once all teams had finished, our facilitator reminded us all, that the task was to get all the blindfolded people to the finishing line. The successful teams should have thought to help others that were struggling. If they had, we'd all have finished the exercise sooner, and got to the bar much more quickly!

What are we doing as a united country to get us back in the pubs? There's division everywhere. Some have complained when they weren't given notice of rule changes. When we were given notice, some claimed the situation could change, and so early action wasn't merited and was detrimental. If we weren't given notice, some understandably said they hadn't been able to plan, which made lives more difficult. The suffering by so many is almost immeasurable and is ongoing. Sadly, there could never be one solution that would satisfy all of us all the time.

23.05

I've just watched the first two episodes of *It's a Sin*. It's set in the early 1980s as the nation first became exposed to, and aware of AIDS and the HIV virus. The characters include conspiracy theorists claiming scientists are spreading virus concerns, so that the scientists can profit from selling medicine. There are people in denial they could ever catch it or give it to anyone else. Some are living in fear and dread that they may already have it or may catch it, no matter how careful they are. Others are researching and trying to learn more about it from the very limited fact-based information. And there are those who are actively trying to stop the spread of the relatively unknown disease, which will only be successfully done with a combined effort.

If they changed the series so the virus in question was Covid, and wound the fashion forward almost forty years, we probably wouldn't notice any difference from our current situation.

Of course, in the 1980s, there wasn't the same access to opinions which detract us from the facts, and cloud our ability to make accurately informed decisions. I deleted my social media apps and it's understandable to me now, that one of the resilience building tools I have since learned about, is to read fact-based information only. If we don't know how to fly a plane, we don't board and then immediately start telling the pilot how to do his job. We all trust the pilot to know what he's doing without even asking for his qualifications or flying methods. We don't pay to eat in a fine dining restaurant, but go into the kitchen once we've ordered, and show the chefs how we want the food cooked. Why do so many of us willingly ignore Professors Whitty and Vallance, each of whom has more letters after their names, than many of us even have in our own?

They say history repeats itself. We don't even seem to have learnt, almost forty years on from the early 1980s, that any hope or cure will be of absolutely no use if we're already dead! We shouldn't need the brain of Brian May to understand that.

23 January 2021

My friends in Australia have shared some more photos of their three sons, my godchildren. I'm nicknamed their fairy godmother. It's unfortunate that the acronym, FGM, has an alternative and very sinister meaning, and I'm grateful no godchild of mine will ever suffer from it.

The photos are of them playing in their garden in Adelaide under blue skies, showered in glorious sunshine. It's forty-one degrees Celsius in Adelaide.

Leicestershire, on the other hand, is covered in a blanket of snow. The temperature is barely above freezing. It's perfect for getting wrapped up and walking. There's something quite comforting about the crunch of fresh snow under your feet. It's equally comforting to know that after an eight-mile round-trip to the next village and back, we'll enjoy a hot bowl of soup with crusty bread.

13:45

I cannot be trusted.

I've sliced the forefinger on my left hand on the bread knife. Bread and blood aren't ideal! Blood certainly isn't butter.

15:15

I still cannot be trusted.

I've now sliced the forefinger on my right hand on broken glass in the sink plug while washing up. It's my own fault for try-ing to force what I thought was a food remnant down the plug, instead of removing it and putting it in the bin. Had I done that, I wouldn't have rammed my finger on the shard of glass that we hadn't realised was still loitering in the plug from when a glass got broken.

I can't even make a bowl of soup without a double injury. Staying in and protecting the NHS doesn't necessarily follow for me. Thankfully, neither injury is serious enough to need more than a self-administered plaster. My hands are symmetrical again, although a dual impression of ET isn't necessarily the best look for a forty-six-year-old.

I'm happy to take the subliminal message that I should avoid all housework.

16:00

I really need to change the finger recognition on my

phone. The plaster has rendered my print unrecognisable and I'm already getting very frustrated repeatedly typing a PIN. Honestly, it's just six digits to type. Talk about first world problems.

24 January 2021

We're venturing out again, taking care in the slippery conditions. Our hospitals are struggling to cope enough, without being further pressurised by people injuring themselves while exercising.

Safely home. Well done us. Given my recent accident-prone behaviour, I'm grateful for that.

26 January 2021

There's been more than one hundred thousand deaths in the UK within twenty-eight days of a positive Covid test. It's a grim statistic. Thankfully, the UK continues to lead the way with its vaccine roll-out, although that won't be of any consolation to grieving families.

29 January 2021

Mr M's gone to bed early after a poor night's sleep last night. I'm joining him and I've not even finished the wine. I'm a changed woman. Does that mean my menopause is complete?

I certainly haven't had any hot flushes for a few weeks now, come to think of it, which is a relief. I'm convinced only a menopausal woman can sweat so much during the night, and not even wake up until the alarm sounds. By the time I wake up from a severe hot flush, I'm shivering as all my body heat has been used to evaporate the pools of sweat enveloping me. It's miraculous I don't wake up so dehydrated that I look like a cross between a salted slug and Keith Richards.

I assure anyone that thinks horses sweat, men perspire, and women glow, there is nothing glowing about a menopausal hot flush. Mr M cannot comprehend why removing more clothing isn't the solution. He cannot comprehend the feeling of burning from the inside.

It started very early for me, much to the doctor's initial disbelief. Eventually, he accepted that it may be hereditary, and that the medical profession itself believes childless women may enter this phase of staying alive sooner than mothers.

30 January 2021

My left ear is so sore. It's my own fault for repiercing a closed hole by forcing an earring through it. Have I dived out of the menopausal pool of sweat straight into a mid-life crisis? Why is it called a crisis anyway? The Oxford English Dictionary definition of crisis is a crucial stage or turning point, an unstable period, a sudden change. Eight years of hot flushes is hardly sudden. Mid-life not giving a shit about what other people think, doesn't roll off the tongue so easily though.

I wasn't allowed to have my ears pierced until I was sixteen. By the time I was twenty-one, in addition to the pair of piercings I got on my sixteenth birthday, I'd had two more courtesy of a professional, and had made another eight holes of my own using a needle. I didn't ice my lobes or bite on a towel. I just pushed a needle through my flesh and then filled the hole with an earring, usually skull or skeleton shaped. I even pierced my own belly button. It smarted.

No doubt any counsellor could earn a decent living analysing why I chose to self-inflict pain in this way. I know now I was, in part, trying to distract myself from other pain I didn't want to face when I was sixteen. At forty-six however, I just like wearing earrings. Thankfully I don't need anyone else's permission or opinion.

Hopefully tonight's live comedy stream can distract me from the pain I feel in the top of my ear.

31 January 2021

What a brilliant night last night. For the first time, Just the

Tonic, the organisation behind several comedy venues around the country, streamed live stand-up to a zoom audience. Russell Kane was the headline act and was his usual energetic self.

SB is not enjoying this morning quite so much and needs to clear his head of the aftermath of the drinks we consumed to help wash down the laughter. We're going to repeat one of last weekend's walks to nearby Market Bosworth and back. The village pub is doing takeaway hot drinks and rolls so I'm already looking forward to a chip butty.

Market Bosworth is famous for the battle there on 22 August 1485, the last significant battle of the Wars of the Roses and won by the Lancastrians. In summer especially, the village can swarm with tourists. Obviously at the moment, as with the rest of the country, the quaint cobbled centre has only slightly more life than the Dead Sea.

It's not the only spot in Leicestershire worthy of a visit. I'm still discovering all that the county has to offer. Apparently, it's the birthplace of our current English language. It's believed that the warring Anglo-Saxons and Vikings set aside their differences around one thousand years ago, and started to share their trades and languages, thus shaping modern English. I'm fairly certain it wouldn't have had innit tagged to the end of every sentence, a trait which also seems to have emanated from here.

Leicester itself dates from before the battle. It's one of the UK's oldest cities and has been occupied for over two thousand years. Not surprisingly, it had its own roman baths, although they're dry nowadays. Some also claim rugby was born out of the bottle-kicking that takes place every Easter in the village of Hallaton.

Leicestershire's got the biggest crisp factory in the world, producing seven million packs a day. It looks like some of our locals eat more than their share. I doubt, though, that they contributed to the three hundred and thirty-five kilograms of Leicester's Daniel Lambert, Britain's fattest man. Gary Lineker has been the face of those crisp adverts, and his own family still has a stall in what has been the biggest covered market in

Europe.

Leicester has the largest Diwali celebrations outside of India, and I heard once our residents represented more religions than in London. Sadly, not everyone appreciates the benefits such diversity can bring. I've witnessed verbal attacks against locals because their skin isn't white. I'm in the other camp. I love the variety so many different cultures bring. Our annual Caribbean carnival is the largest in the UK outside Notting Hill. I used to watch, dumb struck, by those intricately decorated floats, as they passed down Granby Street.

BBC radio Leicester was the first ever local radio station, first broadcast in November 1967. Years earlier, Alice Hawkins campaigned for votes for women and became one of the leading suffragettes. She was originally from Stafford but became a Leicestershire boot and shoe machinist from thirteen years old.

Since then, our nation has benefitted from other Leicestershire-born celebrities. They include Serge and Tom of Kasabian, Easy Life, the Attenborough brothers, Gok Wan, Gordon Banks, John Deacon, Sue Townsend, Mark Selby, Showaddywaddy, Engelbert Humperdink and Rosemary Conley.

The county's folk have helped shape sport, music, fashion, literature, broadcasting and film making, and science. In 1984 while at the University of Leicester, Sir Alec John Jeffreys discovered a method showing variations between individuals' DNA and so invented and developed techniques for genetic fingerprinting and DNA profiling. Apparently, he had a eureka moment while in his Leicester lab. Of course, such moments derive from what Archimedes said when he stepped into a bath, and realised that objects placed in water displaced the same volume of water as the volume of the object itself. Sir Alec isn't from Greece, like Archimedes. Sir Alec was born in England, Oxford to be precise. But it was at Leicester Uni that he and his team had this major scientific breakthrough. And continuing the theme of Leicestershire's contribution to the sciences, The National Space Centre attracts school tours and visitors throughout the entire year.

Nestled in the Midlands, Leicestershire is surrounded by some stunning countryside, and is only sixty-five minutes by train from London, with a transport network that can take you to the corners of the earth. It's also one of only three counties that makes Stilton, together with Derbyshire and Nottingham-shire. Leicestershire is awesome.

Soccer fans everywhere wouldn't talk about Leicester without remembering that our football team won the premier-ship in the 2015-2016 season. A bookmaker laughed at one of our village residents who placed a bet when the odds were five thousand to one. He laughed more than the bookie when he won about sixteen thousand pounds. Hopefully our current team will beat Leeds this afternoon.

13:55

We were back from our walk just in time for the match.

I needed a quick change out of the walking trousers so just grabbed last night's jeans. After an equally quick pee before the game started, I was just about to flush but was panic- stricken by a sea of black in the bowl. It can't be blood, can it? It's solid ebony. What's wrong with me?

Panic over. The black sea is yesterday's knickers. They must still have been stuffed in my jeans.

Leeds won. Boo.

FEBRUARY 2021

2 February 2021

Damn you Billy for waking me at 02:35.

03:40

I am still awake! According to last week's webinar about sleep, it's better if I get up than lie in bed restless. Apparently, waking a few times a night for five or ten minutes is common, and doesn't adversely impact on sleep quality. Conversely, lying in bed may cause my brain to associate bed with restlessness, and make it a regular pattern of behaviour. I've got up.

09:00

I have already done five hours of work. I feel refreshed, cognitive, and productive.

15:00

I am so tired. I need to go for a walk to liven up.
I timed that badly. It absolutely lashed it down and I am soaked. I'm off for a second soak in the bath.

16:45

Rest in peace, Captain, Sir Tom Moore. Thank you for raising spirits, bringing hope, and spreading love.
Only yesterday, the military in Myanmar where you

served in WWII, seized control in a coup d'état. How ironic it features in our news this week.

You fought for us all, and survived WWII. In the only war I have experienced, a war against a global pandemic, you brought our nation's spirit to life and raised around thirty-three million pounds for NHS charities, surpassing your one-thousand-pound target.

You will forever remain in history as a shining beacon of 2020. Rest in peace, Captain Tom. Rest in deserved peace.

3 February 2021

I cannot find my watch.

It's not on my bedside table where I usually leave it. I must have knocked it to the floor in my sleep.

It is not on the floor or under the bed.

I've found it. I'd already put it on. I've done the same with my glasses before, looking for them while already wearing them. I should realise I have them on, as I can't see to look for anything unless I am wearing my visual aids.

The tributes to Captain Tom rightly adorn our front pages and news. Even posthumously, his story brings joy to hearts everywhere.

Conversely, a friend told me how she'd watched a program last night about Michael Ryan. When he was twenty-seven, the handyman randomly shot sixteen people dead at various locations including a school. That incident is now known as the Hungerford massacre of 1987.

I couldn't believe thirteen years had passed. Which is probably because it hasn't been thirteen years. It's been thirty-three years. How embarrassing that I, a business advisor, can't add up to thirty-three. I genuinely and momentarily believed it was 2001. How could I possibly think the year of 9/11, was current? What is wrong with me?

2001 saw a war on terror. 2021 is experiencing a war against a pandemic. It's a different kind of terror than that of

2001, and one we may be more likely to defeat. There's been over ten million vaccines in the UK, including five hundred thousand second doses. There must be so many people that deserve thanks and credit.

4 February 2021

Why am I so tearful? I honestly don't know and wish I did. Then I could fix it. That's how my brain works. If something is broken, then fix it. I'm not broken, am I? Babies cry all the time, and no one suggests they are broken. Why can't I cry without feeling somehow inferior, imbalanced, or broken? I'm not something in *The Repair Shop* waiting for a bit of wood glue.

Is labelling every sentiment helpful? I've read that cases of anxiety in children are increasing. I wonder if that is, at least in part, attributable to the fact that we have only relatively recently started to label certain sentiments as anxiety.

Every person will face challenges throughout life, including children. Our children's challenges will have similarities to those of their parents. Those challenges may have adapted and mutated, like a virus. We used to get bullied at school and children now get trolled on social media. I don't remember children being diagnosed as anxious or depressed. It was life. It passed. Nowadays, a teenage girl can't have mood swings that have been around since Methusela without being carted off for some anxiety therapy. Maybe our children will be better placed to cope with adulthood, by virtue of receiving early therapy.

A lot of adults seem so ill-equipped to cope at present. Sales of alcohol have massively increased. Would adults be coping better if we'd had more therapy as children? Perhaps it's positive that we send children to therapy.

Then again, a lot of children are currently being home-schooled by potential if not actual alcoholics, so they could still end up nervous wrecks when older, regardless of any teenage therapy.

5 February 2021

Hinckley and Bosworth Council has had so many volunteers to help administer vaccines, that registrations have been suspended. It's amazing. The government set a target of fifteen million vaccines to have been administered by mid-February. There's around four hundred thousand being given per day. We may just reach the target, but we wouldn't do so without all the volunteers, willing to stick needles in strangers' arms.

The government seems to have bought enough vaccines for us all to be immunised four times. Of course, some batches always get spoiled, so must be disposed of. We'd be quick to criticise if we didn't have enough, but how long will it be before the questions start about what appears to be stock piling at huge cost?

The Six Nations starts tomorrow. Can England be victorious again? We must beat Scotland in tomorrow's game first. Defeat to our neighbours is not an option. It's fine not to win overall, but we must beat the Scots.

6 February 2021.

6-11. England lost to Scotland. Through no fault of their own, several players haven't played games recently, and understandably they struggled. Some looked unfit and overweight.

Scotland can gloat about the victory, but a five-point margin in the circumstances is hardly a foundation for the Grand Slam.

Despite the defeat, I'm thankful to be able to watch any sport at all. It's credit to so many people that professional sport can be played.

Our cricket team is performing well in India after a series win in Sri Lanka. Joe Root, the England cricket captain, has been getting advice and support from a psychologist. Root wanted to know why he'd often score fifty runs, but then not reach one hundred. He's scored recent double centuries, so it's not unrea-

sonable to conclude the psychological support is reaping benefits.

It makes sense that looking after our brains, the central
processing unit that controls all other parts of our body, will
have a positive impact. I'm gobsmacked that not all professional
athletes have their own psychologist, alongside any coach that
helps build their physical fitness.

I had to come to bed before Mr M. I may be ten years
younger, but I sleep as if I am a decade older. He was obviously
missing me though. Before I had fallen asleep, Alexa chirped up
as Hubby's voice spoke to me from the kitchen asking if I'd like
a little drink of Baileys. Have we met? Yes, I would like one, but
don't dare bring anything less than at least four pub measures.

7 February 2021

Mr M was up hours ago. He wanted some porridge but said
he was worried the microwave ping may wake me, so he had
cornflakes instead. That's so kind of him. I don't know why he
thought five decibels could do what a 5.5 Richter scale earth-
quake in Chile couldn't do in 2005, as I lay in my bunk sleeping
soundly during the tremors.

My best friend has done an hour on her cross trainer. I've
done an hour on the sofa. I killed off more brain cells last night
and need to clear my head, although it's a bit late now for anything longer than a walk around our own village.

That wind is bitter. I'm thankful for warm clothing as it's
certainly helped to get out in the air, even if it is baltic. There
are signs of spring coming. The days are lengthening and our
tubs by the front door have started to sprout from the bulbs we
planted.

More than twelve million people in the UK have had their
first vaccine. That's about a fifth of our population in a matter of
weeks. It's remarkable.

8 February 2021

The naval gazing about England's defeat by Scotland continues. Our nation's armchair experts are criticising the team selection choices.

Simultaneously, England's cricket captain is being chastised for not declaring sooner in the test against India. Root, who's been scoring runs for fun and knows his players and their capabilities, has made his decision. That's his job. I sincerely hope we take the nine wickets needed for victory tomorrow, not only to secure the win but also to absolve our captain.

Of course, if we don't win tomorrow, we will never know if an earlier declaration may have avoided a draw. Root's done what he thinks gives our team the best chance to win. He doesn't come into our working environments and question us. I have faith in that decision and in our bowlers.

Even worse, Mike Dean, the professional football referee has received death threats following two decisions to send off players. Both decisions were overturned, but no matter how poor the decisions may have been, a death threat can't ever be a proportionate response.

If anyone in my team at work makes a mistake, we help put it right. We offer apologies where needed and consider whether changes are needed to avoid recurrences. We wouldn't accept anyone in our workplace being subject to any abuse.

It's unfortunate that those issuing death threats against Mr Dean may have got what they wanted. He's asked to step down, at least temporarily, from refereeing some matches. I don't blame him but hope he returns soon. I just hope it's not to referee Leicester's next match.

I wondered some months ago if it was appropriate to allow professional sport to recommence. I may be biased by my own enjoyment, but I'm persuaded that the benefits for players and supporters justify it. I don't struggle to entertain myself but I'm grateful to be able to watch two rugby matches, two football matches and some cricket this weekend.

One of my work friends has secured a place to run in this

year's London marathon after trying for twelve years, which reminds me it's time to run my bath.

9 February 2021

Oh Jimmy, Jimmy!
Jimmy, Jimmy, Jimmy, Jimmy Anderson!
England easily won the first test in India. That should quieten those that criticised the timing of Root's declaration.

Similarly, those that said Jimmy was too old to keep bowling need to put fingers on lips. He's taken three hundred and forty-three wickets in the eight years since he turned thirty. That's seventy-five more than the two hundred and sixty-eight he took in the eleven-year test career period before that milestone birthday.

Of England's top eight test wicket takers, Jimmy, since turning thirty, is third behind Stuart Broad with five hundred and seventeen wickets, and Sir Ian Botham with three hundred and eighty-three. Pre-thirty-year-old Jimmy sits between Graeme Swann with two hundred and fifty-five, and Derek Underwood with two hundred and ninety-seven. They're behind Fred Trueman on three hundred and seven, and Bob Willis with three hundred and twenty-five.

In his entire career, Jimmy, aged thirty-eight, (and over the hill according to some), tops that leader board with six hundred and eleven wickets. He's a legend.

I accept and understand why not everyone shares my passion for cricket. For some, five days of cricket that may end in a draw doesn't compute. A series of an odd number of matches that can end in a draw, leaves some scratching their heads.

On the other hand, I'm astounded by the mental agility and concentration levels that cricketers demonstrate. The only thing I seem to be able to focus on for five days is watching a cricket test match.

13:55

Snow across the country is impeding our vaccine roll-out. Numerous centres have understandably closed for safety reasons. Despite this, 12.6 million in the UK have had their first dose. Our NHS continues to implore people not to go out unnecessarily, as accidents may happen requiring hospital treatment. Would anyone that needs to go to hospital to be treated after an injury suffered while unnecessarily outside, benefit from a simultaneous lobotomy? Could we future proof our country very cost efficiently against stupidity?

14:45

I've left my phone somewhere.

14:48

It's in the drawer from where I removed an address book when ordering a friend's birthday card. Of course, if I did what Hubby suggested, and put the addresses in my phone like a normal forty-six-year-old with an eight-hundred-pound phone, it wouldn't have happened. My problem is that I am a technophobe. I don't get excited by new IT equipment. I'd rather pee in my eye than set up a new phone or laptop.

I received my new laptop from work eight days ago. It is still in the box. I already have one that works. I recall being taught not to fix what isn't broken. Well, just like spontaneously tearful me, my laptop isn't broken.

We've ordered some meat from a new supplier and it arrived today. The driver immediately apologised for being later than notified. I hadn't even given it a second thought. We don't go anywhere other than for walks. He told us he'd just forgotten to stop by, as we're a new customer. He could have blamed his tardiness on the icy conditions and snow, and I'd have believed him. More of this honesty, I say. I forgive that delivery driver for his mistake, and I welcome his candour.

10 February 2021

What beautiful blue skies looking down on the white snow.

I'm under strict instructions from Mr M not to immediately don the freshly ironed clothes.

I've not finished my tea and now it's too cold even for me to enjoy. Thank goodness for microwaves. I've found a mug in the microwave, with about an inch of coffee in that I wanted to reheat earlier. I need to finish my drinks.

It's wine Wednesday and there's more footy tonight. Leicester play Brighton in the FA Cup. Oh no! Mike Dean is the referee. I finished the wine just as Leicester scored in the final moments. Bed!

12 February 2021

The end of another week brought news of the outcome of a complaint I raised months ago.

Last September, I complained to one of America's Big Five IT companies. I'd bought a new phone in August 2018 and was persuaded by the salesman to buy the after-care insurance product for an extra one hundred and twenty-nine pounds.

I only bought it as he promised me a full and automatic refund into my bank account if I didn't claim under the insurance policy in the two-year period for which it was valid. I didn't receive the refund, so rang to claim it. Bring on Cilla Black. Surprise Surprise, it's a non-refundable policy. Anyone that knows me would not be surprised that I complained. Credit where it's due, but I won't tolerate poor service or lies.

I heard nothing from the giant corporate. Like David against Goliath, I persevered. I spent hours holding on the phone. Then I put pen to paper and when I still didn't get a reply, I emailed the CEO.

Drum roll for the result! I'm being fully refunded for the mis-sold product. In addition, as a gesture of goodwill, I can buy a product up to the cost of two hundred pounds and will be contacted about this soon.

Hubby always says that any complaint gives an organisation an opportunity to demonstrate how much it values customers. Mistakes happen, and in this instance, there have been several. Nevertheless, as I sit in the kitchen eating my breakfast reading this email, I feel satisfied by the outcome.

I've also just noticed that we need to buy more fruit. After all, Mum always said I should eat an apple a day.

13 February 2021

My former employer's chairman resigned yesterday after complaints about comments he made to around fifteen hundred employees. I'm grateful for work, but I empathise with so many of those employees who said they were drained. The chairman's response that they should "Stop moaning" and work harder has ironically left him out of work.

In challenging times, good leaders take steps to protect their people, as well as their business. Without the first, you lose the second.

Our entire nation, working or not, is exhausted. I'm thankful I can buy an extra week's annual leave by sacrificing some of my salary. I've never done it before, and although I'm unlikely to venture abroad, this year more than ever before, I need more time off work.

14 February 2021

The cricket hasn't gone well on a shambles of a wicket that has more cracks than a sumo wrestling tournament.

11:05

We've decided to get out in the fresh air before the forecast rain comes. It will also delay when we start drinking the fizz we have reserved for today.

Some people really go to town on Valentine's Day. We don't, but we buy each other a card and a small gift. Even if we didn't normally, I think we'd have made an exception this year.

I've never forgotten all the years I spent without a partner. I didn't receive cards or gifts, but I always tried to be thankful for the benefits of being single. I know that today won't be a happy day for some.

Conversely, I'm overjoyed that Hubby has treated me to a Jo Malone candle. We've also roared with laughter at his very apt choice of card which reads, "Happy Valentine's blah blah blah wine."

I've just read that the Jo Malone company founder left school at thirteen to care for her mother who'd suffered a stroke. Ms Malone opened her first store in 1994 aged thirty-one. Five years later, she sold the company to Estée Lauder for undisclosed millions. Well done, Jo.

Everyone I have told about my gift raves about the products. I've been looking at the website, and I draw the line at the candle you can buy for three hundred and twenty pounds. That's wax, in a glass jar!

I might as well just get a wad of tenners and see how they fare against a lit match if I've got that amount of money to burn.

Some things I just cannot bring myself to buy. Three-hundred-and-twenty-pound candles are one, and Sheese is another. Sheese has just been advertised on TV as cheese, only vegan. It's not cheese then, is it? Isn't it like those tofu treats purporting to be sausages? It sounds like it could be a breach of the Trade Descriptions Act 1968, but I wasn't very good at my degree, so what would I know? Carnivores may claim tofu and treat don't belong in the same sentence without being an oxymoron.

Thankfully, we're allowed to make personal choices. I'm not going to buy any household fragrant product that costs three figures and disappears before your eyes. I'm also not going to buy Sheese, or anything else that sounds, to me, like a female urinating device, but is supposed to be edible.

I will also never buy fabric softener that is in black packaging. I know it's totally illogical. I favour black as a fashion choice as it makes it easy to get dressed without risking clashing colours. But it isn't appealing as fabric softener packaging. It's associated with death, plague, witches, and Black Sabbath. It doesn't induce thoughts of lambs gambolling amongst pastel-coloured croci, or of snuggling in a duvet, as softener should. I've no idea which marketing guru came up with the idea, but I would love to know how sales of it compare.

16 February 2021

Hubby's birthday

We planned to spend last weekend at The George of Stamford, but we had a great time together at home instead. We will enjoy today as best as we can on a Tuesday during a pandemic. We won't get any of this time back so it's wasteful to waste it on regrets.

Mr M insisted he cook his birthday meal choice, a venison haunch. I know not to argue, so in a vague attempt at a team effort, I peeled the spuds and poured some wine.

17 February 2021

I decided to do some typing in the kitchen after work and noted that the keys keep sticking. I told Hubby that it strangely only ever happens when I leave the study.

SB pointed out that I use a separate keyboard when I'm in the study, as the laptop sits closed on the hub. Whoops. Amoeba-brain strikes again.

19:15

I managed to cook a delicious pork stir-fry, a recipe from a well-known organisation that promotes itself as the "Nation's favourite way to lose weight." Its website says there's "No weighing, no measuring and no counting calories."

This brag seems odd at best. Each recipe has a list of ingredients, with associated quantities, and a method. Tonight's recipe doesn't say I should chuck in as much pork mince as I feel like and soak it with as many pints of soy as takes my fancy. It's all weighed, or measured, or counted.

It's also supposed to serve four people. Hubby and I ate it, all, partly because it's delicious, and partly because it only serves two adults with stomachs.

Mr M ate these recipes religiously a few years ago. He drank alcohol at weekends and didn't exercise any more than he did before. He ate as much food as he wanted and lost two stone.

He follows a different weight management regime now. We still enjoy some of those previous regime recipes for four, but I wonder who these people are, that eat portions the size of my five-year-old self.

18 February 2021

I've decided to defrost some of the frozen mixed fruit we ordered this week, to enjoy in my morning smoothie with a banana. I have found a mug in the microwave, again. It had a bit of tea left in it. That's the mug I put in the microwave after removing a mug that had a bit of coffee in it. For goodness' sake. I need smaller mugs.

19 February 2021

Perseverance rover has landed on Mars. It's taken around seven months to get there and will spend two years looking for evidence of past life. The mission was announced by NASA on 4 December 2012 and NASA will have invested roughly US$2.8 billion over ten years.

Meanwhile, back on Planet Earth trying to save existing lives, the volunteers, NHS, Department of Health, and Health Secretary, amongst so many others, continue with the biggest vaccination roll-out the UK has ever delivered. Every UK adult could receive both jabs by the end of August.

I have needed the services of several healthcare systems abroad, and I have yet to find any as good as our NHS. No doubt, improvements can be made. I've worked with some of our trusts throughout my career and I'm certain there continues to be huge amounts of wasted resource. But I believe this roll-out is second to none, and I haven't read any reports of any country doing it any better.

20 February 2021

Crap! I've slept eleven hours and woken to realise it's been five weeks since I washed the bed linen. I pity our wall planner that only records laundry rotas. Perhaps I should start recording our moments of excitement.

Then again, the current excitement benchmark isn't necessarily one I want to document. I've told all our friends that Mr M can hardly contain his joy about a soft close toilet lid that snaps in place on the bowl, allowing easy removal. He's excited because he doesn't have to go on bended knee to reach underneath the toilet to secure the fittings.

I'm excited because cleaning the entire unit will be so much easier. Over the years, I've spent umpteen hours I won't get back, pushing cleaning cloth corners or old toothbrushes into nooks and crannies, in a vain attempt to remove every grain of dirt. Thankfully, we have found a time-saving lid.

Similarly, the bulldog clip trick when making the bed worked again. Such excitement! I can barely control myself and feel I must lie down. No, Annabelle, don't lie down and ruin the bed you've just made.

The Leicester Tigers' win against Wasps is an equally great result today. There's more local rivalry between those clubs since Wasps moved from the team's London stadium a few years ago, to play at the Ricoh Stadium in Coventry at the other end of the M69.

I enjoy the passion and support fans show for a local team. We have friends who enjoy rugby union too, and they support

Wasps. We've just spoken, and after today's game, we'll be adult enough to hug and kiss and remain friends, regardless of the result. But I struggle with the animosity that some fans display, including fans of the round ball game. We will respect that neither team could play competitively without an opponent, and will be thankful all teams exist. Of course, we won't be hugging after today's game, but that's because of a pandemic.

17:55

I spoke to my sister who's at the end of her half term week. It's worrying that she only seems slightly less tired than she was before it started. She's not done any schoolwork at all, a very rare but necessary occurrence. The increasing frequency of her migraines may be proportionate to the deterioration in her eyesight.

As children, when Mum dropped a needle on the floor while darning our holey school jumpers, we'd ask Sis to find it. I'm sure she could find a needle in a haystack. Meanwhile, I need a Hubble telescope to find my glasses.

During this pandemic, my sister's eyesight has required visual aids for the first time. She's sensibly avoided screens as much as possible over half term, as our nation degenerates into myopic alcoholics.

For anyone trying to decide on a career path, I suggest optometry or counselling.

22:55

I was just about to go upstairs after the last of my Bay Leaves, (as I now call it after the faux pas order with Alexa), when we both heard a bang and crash of glass that brought back horrific memories of my numerous car crashes.

I wanted to check our CCTV and call the police. We spent over four figures a year ago on the former, and we pay for the latter via taxes. Mr M, on the other hand, was already out of the kitchen and headed for the front door. As I tried dragging him back to the kitchen, he tried to convince me nothing was awry. In the end, I let him continue with me in tow. It turns out that when I'm panic-stricken, I can't function well enough to look at the CCTV footage on my phone anyway. Why did we buy it?

Ground floor, clear.

First floor. A honeymoon photo had fallen off the landing wall. We weren't being burgled. We just have a lemming photo, or poltergeists!

Coincidentally today, our local police force sent a burglary update to anyone who'd registered to receive them. Across fifty-two local villages, in 2021 so far, there have been just two burglaries. In both instances, the suspects have been apprehended. The police recognise the low burglary numbers are partly due to our current lockdown, but it's a welcome, perfect record of burglary solving. I can't comment on poltergeist numbers, other than they may have increased by one.

21 February 2021

We've not got poltergeists. This morning, I recalled removing the wall picture to clean it, and I must not have rehung it properly. I've taken this as another sign that I should ditch any housework.

I know I'm grasping for any excuse to avoid chores, just as I cling onto the hope the vaccine is bringing. Is either wrong? I feel better. In fact, I feel positive, with good reason. Our PM wants all adults to have their first vaccine by the end of July! That's only sixteen months after the first lockdown, and less than the usual minimum two-year period to develop a vaccine, let alone administer it.

Our Health Secretary has been found guilty of breaking the law that requires publicity within thirty days of any contract awarded that may cost the public pursue more than one hundred and twenty thousand pounds. Mr Hancock and his team have worked eighteen-hour days, seven days a week, securing PPE to save lives. He missed a thirty-day deadline by just over two weeks. The law is the law, and he broke it. He broke it prioritising saving lives. The law can be such an ass.

At uni, as with most of the law students, I was childishly engaged by the R v Brown case. In 1993, the House of Lords, (now Supreme Court), reaffirmed an earlier conviction of five men for their involvement in consensual sadomasochistic sexual acts. Despite consenting, those men were convicted of various offences including actual bodily harm. In a bare majority decision where three out of five judges found against the men, the judges found that cruelty is uncivilised. They found it wasn't in the public interest that the acts be found lawful.

How could it be in our public interest that Mr Hancock and his team divert their resources to prioritise publicising details of signed contracts, ahead of saving lives? Would our nation not reasonably have accused him of having incorrect priorities if he'd done the opposite? Mr Hancock and his team broke the law, at risk of being found guilty of an offence, to put our lives above their own. Of the choices that have been made, should that be one we criticise?

22 February 2021

Our PM has announced his roadmap back to freedom. It feels like a Nelson Mandela story. Hopefully liberation won't take twenty-five years.

The journalists continued their quest to ask the same question several times using different semantics, knowing it couldn't be answered.

Professor Whitty, we know you don't like predicting numbers, but how many people will die?

Mr M and I turn off before a particular journalist wins the record for being the most annoying person on the planet.

A friend of mine suggested a solution to anyone's dislike of the media, and to our fishermen's woes. Each person annoyed with a journalist could buy one fish, then stand in a socially distanced queue and take turns to slap a journalist. My friend said this could negate the reduction in fish sales since the EU stopped our fishermen selling to EU countries and we'd kill two birds with one stone. Or rather, we'd each slightly tickle one journalist with a gill-bearing animal. Like the fish, I'm not convinced the idea has legs.

We could be allowed to meet up to thirty people outdoors as early as from 17 May. Sadly, my parent's golden wedding anniversary celebrations on Sunday 9 May 2021 will need to be postponed. If that's the worst that happens to our family, we'll all be very thankful.

The PM has said that social contact limits in England could be over from 21 June 2021, the longest day of the year. I have just checked to see if I could book that week off work, but I already have client commitments. It's probably no bad thing, judging by people's behaviours after previous rule relaxations.

23 February 2021

Hubby and I had an impromptu movie night because we found two films we wanted to watch.

In the first, *The Confirmation*, Clive Owen played a divorced father and recovering alcoholic, out of permanent work, and caring for his son at weekends.

The second, *I Care a Lot*, starred Rosamund Pike as a businesswoman, Marla Grayson. The US courts would appoint Grayson as legal guardian over elderly and wealthy patients deemed unfit to care for themselves. An unscrupulous doctor would manipulate the facts so that the witness statements supported the unnecessary cases for a guardian to be appointed over the doctor's patients. Then Grayson would drain their savings. My blood was boiling.

Both main characters in each film were charged with caring for someone else. Ironically, the one that seemed the least fit to do so, was better equipped because he was driven by genuine love for his son, and not greed. Grayson got what many would feel she deserved, but not before irreparable damage and pain had been inflicted on innocent families. It could have been a metaphor for so many situations.

24 February 2021

Our neighbour has messaged us, "Black bins matter. Have you put yours out?"

Oops. No, we haven't.

We all know that neither our neighbour nor we, are be-littling or ignoring the garden waste bin or recycling. They had their time last week and will do so again next week. But if we don't give the black bin an outing down the cul-de-sac, it'll be a month between being emptied. Thank goodness for observant neighbours.

It's my sister-in-law's silver wedding anniversary today. Mr M walked her down the aisle twenty-five years ago. I'm de-lighted she's with a wonderful man who respects and honours her, and with whom she is creating happy memories. Mr M and her didn't have happy childhoods. She was inwardly pleased when her father hurt his foot and couldn't give her away. None of us can undo those unhappy times, but we can all continue to create better memories now.

When hospitality venues can reopen, we shall treat them to a belated, celebratory champagne breakfast. Why is it OK to drink champagne at nine o'clock in the morning but if I opened a bottle of Sauvignon Blanc, Hubby would probably be ringing the doctor to get help for his alcoholic wife? It is OK to drink cham-pagne at nine o'clock, isn't it?

25 February 2021

SB has been playing with my new earpieces, sent to me courtesy of the US IT giant against whom I lodged a complaint. We couldn't get them to work last night which almost led to an-other complaint.

The cricket test in India has ended in a dismal defeat for England in two days out of a possible five. I've never known a potential five-day test to have play on only two days, other than when rain has prevented more. The International Cricket Council probably won't do anything about the atrocious wicket. That pot-holed pitch didn't produce more than one hundred and forty-five runs in any of the four innings, each of which was less than fifty-five overs. The test match has done nothing other than fuel the argument to shorten five-day test matches. As I moaned about it to a friend, he warned me to keep quiet before someone starts a Crap Pitches Matter movement.

On the plus side, cricket being played abroad means that spring is coming to the UK. Hugs are also coming. It's only ten months to Christmas.

Our Queen has had a video call with those coordinating the vaccine roll-out across the UK. She said the vaccine didn't hurt at all. Her Majesty never publicly talks about her health, which is why this otherwise unsurprising announcement is newsworthy.

A jab doesn't hurt. Pain may come from rare horrendous side effects, or long-term damage akin to the thalidomide tragedy of the 1960s, but a jab in itself doesn't hurt. In some situations, a reasonably sized prick is very welcome. Of course, Her Majesty would never speak publicly of that.

26 February 2021

I sponsored a friend today who will walk ten thousand steps a day in March to raise money for life-saving cancer research. SB and I have chosen various charities to which we already donate, so we don't normally sponsor anyone, or ask for sponsorship if we embark on anything that could raise awareness. Occasionally, I make an exception, like today. It's no more than I'd happily have spent in a pub on a Friday, so I am pleased to be able to give more to charities.

Stupidly I gave less than I'd intended because someone else at work had also donated. I was concerned they'd see my donation and think I was trying to upstage them. The charity will receive less money because I have an irrational fear. I am a prick. And not a welcome one.

There's been over nineteen million very welcome pricks.

27 February 2021

The views from our bedroom window across the fields at the back of our house are stunning. Spring has sprung today, and as the tree leaves aren't yet in bloom, we can see all the way to the next village. We walked in the opposite direction for four miles and had a pit-stop at the village cob shop.

Mr M wanted a sausage and tomato torpedo. I forgot what he asked for. It couldn't have been much more than five seconds between him telling me, and me standing at the shop counter. I had to leave the shop and ask him again. I apologised to the shopkeeper that at the age of forty-six, I had become my seventy-three-year-old forgetful mother.

Hubby and I got chatting to a lady outside who had her first child a month ago. She saw our rugby tops and asked, "Are you on your way to the match?"

Not wanting to be rude to a stranger, Hubby told her we were walking home in time for it to be shown on TV at one o'clock. At this point, she realised her mistake, and promptly blamed her baby brain.

18:45

I'm not entirely surprised that the Tigers lost to the top of the table, or that England lost to Wales in the Six Nations. But the refereeing by Pascal Gaüzère was quite shocking. Some would argue it wasn't even that good, and others would say it cost England the game.

In truth, the team wasn't good enough, and our lack of discipline was as costly as the poor refereeing decisions. We could have beaten fifteen Welsh players, a referee, two touch judges and a fourth match official, if we'd kept our heads. As it was, a team of fifteen conceding far too many penalties against nineteen people, wasn't ever going to be victorious.

It wasn't long before jokes started to circulate. A friend sent me what was supposedly a tweet by Specsavers. It asked, "Who is Pascal Gaüzère, and why are hundreds of people trying to book him an eye test?"

Mr M and I made our own laughter, after seeing an advert for a popular medicine used to treat thrush. We made our own rhyming slogans, but Hubby was laughing so much he couldn't say his for a while. I was then in fits before I'd even heard what he was about to say. How can I be this childish while simultaneously going through the menopause?

28 February 2021

SB cleaned his car while I walked around our village. I christened my new earpieces and spoke to both my folks. Mum and I spent most of our chat comparing menopause symptoms which had us both in stitches. I can picture her now, holding her stomach and crossing her legs in an attempt not to leak. I'm not yet at that stage, but I am as forgetful and as clumsy. It's annoying enough going into a room and forgetting what you went in for. But banging yourself on door frames while sober, like an adult pinball game, takes the mick.

This weekend's results have gone in threes with today's Leicester City defeat to Arsenal.

15:40

I have cleared all the creeping ivy off the back fence, ready to spray it with algae killer and then paint it.

Last summer, I spent eight consecutive weekends painting two coats on the right-hand fence. My friends are laughing at how excited I am at the prospect of finer weather allowing me to paint the back fence. It will finish the garden appearance, like having a clean pair of shoes with a smart outfit. Painting a fence is also a pretty good workout, squatting up and down. Double win.

Thanks to all our delivery drivers, I've ordered some paint which will be brought to our front door within a week. I don't even need to tax my car to go and collect it.

21:10

I've just remembered I need to tax my car. I'm going to the dentist next week for the first time in eighteen months. I go every six months normally, but decided it wasn't worth the risks when I wasn't experiencing any oral issues. I haven't driven since September when I attended a funeral.

I was bemoaning the cost of taxing my car to go to the dentist but realised I've saved a fortune over the last year and should stop whining. I'm thankful I'm able to go to the dentist at all.

MARCH 2021

1 March 2021

First day of spring. Or is that 21 March? Why do I not know when our seasons start and end?

2 March 2021

Dentist day

Who are all these people on the roads? It's not even rush hour but feels like it. Have people forgotten we are in lockdown? They're perhaps wondering the same about me.

I had to stop for fuel and saw people rightly wearing masks, but then inexplicably removing them to speak. No doubt Mr M would call them stupid, selfish pricks.

Are these the same people that fly tip their rubbish, without any care or thought of the consequences? Our once beautiful countryside is being decimated. It's embarrassing that people think tipping is acceptable behaviour. It's almost equally embarrassing that most go unpunished, which is partly why this scourge continues. In medieval times, culprits would have been placed in the stocks so that villagers could return their rubbish to them.

Miraculously, the dentist was very pleased with both my teeth and gums. She queried what may be the reason for a reduction in staining compared to my last visit eighteen months ago. I told her it must be due to the reduction in red wine consumption.

She seemed unconvinced. I'm equally doubtful as my

credit card bill includes a well-known online retailer, a well-known online greeting card company, a wine delivery, another wine delivery, aforementioned well-known online retailer, a third wine delivery, yet another wine delivery, yoga class, fifth wine delivery, and sixth wine delivery.

3 March 2021

Budget day

What will 00 Sunak say today?

If our country was a corporate entity, it would need some insolvency advice. Somehow, the country must repay what it's borrowed. I'm not suggesting that the support packages haven't been essential or beneficial, but the loans must be repaid at some point.

I refuse to worry about it. I'm not the Chancellor of the Exchequer. It's not my job to make the UK's books balance. We managed after the world wars, so should be able to do so again.

My talented sister-in-law sent us each a crocheted heart, one predominantly orange and one mostly purple. They came wrapped in a crocheted drawstring bag, accompanied by a bag of cherry chocolates, one of my favourite treats. The hearts now hang on the knobs of the wardrobes by our bed. Mine will be one of the first things I see each morning and I'm sure it will make me smile every day.

I feel the need to pay forward the kindness. Throughout lockdown, we've made soups for those who need food, and sent flowers to elderly relatives. I also sent gin to some friends, as a gift should be what the recipient would appreciate. Our friends don't want flowers or soup.

00 Sunak has, perhaps unnecessarily, told us that tax hikes may come in a few years.

4 March 2021

I treated myself to a designer case for my free earpieces. I made a schoolgirl error telling Hubby that I'd found the designer one on a website for a considerable amount less than on the designer's own webpage. He didn't ask me how much it cost but questioned why I needed it when I'd already got a black rubber one.

"Why are you double bagging the earpieces?"

I'm sure double bagging means something else.

I continued the schoolgirl errors, writing wood instead of would in a message to a friend, and then cool instead of school. Is there any hope for our nation's literacy if a grammar and spelling pedant like me errs?

A friend of ours that lives in Cornwall has just surprised his wife with a bottle of gin. She's trying to cut down so hasn't bought any lately, and isn't keeping tonic in the house. Aaargh! She has one can of diet gin and tonic in the fridge. I don't think she realised I was being serious when I suggested that could be her mixer.

Her situation reminded me of my first Christmas with Mr M, before I was Mrs M. We'd gone to stay at a friend's pub in Devon and so had taken our gifts with us. I'd bought Mr M the zippo lighter he wanted. I also bought him some lighter gas. I was more pleased by that than the zippo, as I was sure Mr M didn't expect to be able to use his new lighter until we'd returned home.

Unfortunately, my pleasure was short-lived as I should have bought lighter fuel, not gas. What an idiot, but we laughed. It's the thought that counts anyway.

Our friend's lack of tonic is my ideal opportunity to pay it forward. My heart is breaking to know that she is being kept from gin, so I've ordered twenty-four cans to be delivered directly to her door. The message reads, "Hide somewhere. For emergencies only! Love AZM".

5 March 2021

The latest government data shows that cases have fallen

by just over a third in the last week. Hospital admissions have also fallen by almost thirty percent, the quickest decrease of any time during the pandemic. Deaths have dropped in the last week by forty-one percent and two-fifths of the adult population in the UK have had their first dose of the vaccine. It's all very encouraging.

My new garden sprayer has arrived. I can finally get the algae killer onto the back fence. I can hardly wait to commence more harmful organism blasting.

Bugger! There's no tonic for my gin.

6 March 2021

I've remembered! Condoms. That's what the term double bagging refers to. Or at least my uni mates would call anyone they thought was a health risk, "a double-bagger". As if having sex was obligatory.

Hubby and I made it to the next village four miles away, twenty minutes before the cob shop closed. Result. I sprayed some of the back fence when we got home, and I've found some tonic in the garage fridge. I've descaled the kettle (not with the tonic). Can today get any better?

I've revisited the job list I wrote at the start of lockdown last year. It has forty-seven items. We've done twenty-two. Unfortunately, some of those completed tasks are recurring items, so the list of twenty-five outstanding jobs will become longer than that.

7 March 2021

My earpiece case is in the Sunday Times Style magazine. I am stylish.

8 March 2021

Primary schools have reopened after more than two months. This must be like manna from heaven for parents. Not that it affects us.

Why did Mr M book his car in for its MOT today, of all days? The school traffic is horrendous.

My red earpiece case clashes with my burgundy jumper, which has yesterday's dinner down the front of it. I have only just noticed the food stain as I am about to cook tonight's curry. I am not stylish.

Tonight is Oprah's interview with the Duke and Duchess of Sussex. Mr M will no doubt say he doesn't care about their lives and hasn't any interest in watching it. But shouldn't we be interested? Our Monarch is the Head of the Church of England, Head of the British Armed Forces and Head of State.

Some may see "the firm" as nothing but an outdated tradition. So is a nine to five job, but millions of people still rely on one. The Royal Family generates huge amounts of income for our United Kingdom. The sovereign grant to support official duties and to maintain Historic Royal Palaces is twenty-five percent of the Crown's estate revenue from the previous two years. HM Treasury (we) get the rest. When I went to school, that meant seventy-five percent, equating to around three hundred and forty-four million pounds. Why do we moan?

The former President of France, Nicolas Sarcozy, has this year been tried and convicted of corruption, amongst other things. He's appealing, which stays his jail sentence. President Trump was impeached. Again! The Monarchy may not be perfect, but what is?

But if anyone should be able to say whether they stay within the institution or not, shouldn't it be the family members that are born into a life of public service and scrutiny? It may be futile, as even after stepping away, it seems unlikely the Sussexes will enjoy a private life.

Which begs the question, what good can come of tonight's interview? They have chosen to step away from a life that attracts incessant attention. They have also chosen to take part in an interview, seemingly to straighten some records. Those records could have been left to be yesterday's old vinyl, forever enveloped in a sleeve, rarely, if ever, to be played again. I don't know of any interview that has successfully changed the views of a divided nation, so that everyone thinks the same after it. I cannot see how any good can come of their interview.

9 March 2021

Piers Morgan has stepped down from Good Morning Britain, which some people will believe is good news. I welcome freedom of speech, but can appreciate that an apparent goal to incite fire-fuelling, may inevitably results in someone's ashes.

Just as Piers will no longer speak to the nation on GMB, I lost the ability to speak mid-sentence during a work zoom meeting this morning. I was so exhausted, I couldn't even think how to finish the sentence I had started. Rarely have I been lost for words.

The only other time I remember was during my first trip back home to Blackburn from being at university in Strasbourg. During dinner one evening, I had forgotten how to say mortgage. I kept repeating the French, hypothèque. My non-francophone parents couldn't comprehend, despite me repeating it more loudly and more slowly than before.

I resorted to digging out my French-English dictionary and proudly announced my mother tongue equivalent. My dad was adamant I was joking. He couldn't believe I could forget my first language. His frustration that he thought his daughter wasn't being entirely truthful was as evident as my own.

I hadn't appreciated then, the brief insight into how midlife would be. Nowadays rarely a day passes when I haven't walked into a room and forgotten why, or forgotten where I put something, or started a sentence without recalling the punchline by the time I get to it.

It's almost non-sensical to be living a slower-paced life but simultaneously being more drained than before. I continue to read rational explanations for our nation's lethargy. During remote online meetings, our brains are working overtime, filling in what we would otherwise see when in person. Our brains are busy trying to make sense of the changes in our life. I wish I could tell my brain not to bother expending its capacity trying to rationalise what it can't control. I'd prefer it to focus on the stuff I need it to do, like remembering, what was it?

10 March 2021

A parcel has arrived filling me with excitement it may be an unexpected birthday gift, over two weeks early. I asked Hubby to open it and stash it away if so. It's the fence paint I forgot I'd ordered.

There's news of human remains found, suspected to be those of a thirty-three-year-old woman who went missing a week ago. A police officer has been arrested. This tragic news comes on the day a two-part documentary starts about the abduction and murder of two-year-old James Bulger, twenty-eight years ago. Two ten-year-olds were arrested and convicted of his abduction, torture, and murder. Two ten-year-olds! Three families lost their child that day. The nation lost the belief of innocence in children.

We need a vaccine for evil it seems. In the meantime, there's been 20,248,632 vaccines against Covid, including 868,272 second doses.

11 March 2021

It's the second part of the documentary about the murder of James Bulger by two ten- year-olds. There's an advert about looking ten years younger in ten days. I can't help feeling that focussing on exterior appearances, is misdirected. Shouldn't we focus on interior health and mentality? Those two young murderers looked naïve and innocent.

12 March 2021

I've tried to make my smoothie without plugging the

blender in, while simultaneously looking like I have electrocuted myself. I suddenly have hair so big that Don King would be impressed. I've never been a princess or a queen, so I may as well be thankful I look like a King.

13 March 2021

I've received another scam email purporting to offer free gifts if I click a link. This time I could receive a Dyson vacuum. I was telling Mr M, but my recent inability to speak wasn't as temporary as I hoped, and it came out as Dacsun vycuum.

Speaking in spoonerisms, malapropisms, and with other slips of the tongue, runs in our family. Grandma and Mum regularly had us in stitches. Coincidentally, Mr M's had a social media reminder from a year ago. I was sitting in the kitchen listening to the radio which was playing Elton John when I declared, "I can't believe Bernie Winters wrote the lyrics before Elton wrote the music!" Once my husband's hysteria had calmed down, he asked me, "Does Schnorbitz play the guitar?" It's Taupin. Bernie Taupin!

14:16

So far today, leek and potato soup has been in the slow cooker for over two hours, chicken and leek pie filling is made for tonight's meal, and pork steaks are marinating in honey and soy for tomorrow's fodder.

It's over two hours since the yard arm was over, and time for a glass of SB!

Perhaps I should get dressed first. Crikey! Rugby starts in less than forty-five minutes.

14 March 2021

A second mothers' day without being with her. I must remain hopeful this restriction is temporary, and that I will, again, see and hug her. So many others haven't the hope that I cling to.

15 March 2021

It's my niece's sixteenth birthday. Such occasions inevitably result in reminiscing. I remember my sister telling me in 2005 she was about to have some time off work. I was selfishly livid that she may be stealing my thunder. I'd not long since told my family I had agreed a six-month career break to travel round parts of South America with my boyfriend. I was certain my sister wasn't going to do the same.

Pregnancy. That's why she was having time off work. To have my niece. I was thrilled, for more than one reason. My sister had always wanted children and I had no doubt she'd be a loving and wonderful mum. It also selfishly took the pressure off me, as I wasn't exactly keen to give my parents any grandchildren.

Great job Sis, and the timing was perfect as my niece came along before I departed the UK for five months, so I was able to meet and hug her before I went. By the time I returned, I too looked like I was pregnant, after overindulging in cheap delicacies every morning, noon, and night. It took me twelve weeks doing one hundred sit-ups per day to shift the twelve pounds I'd gained.

My niece is only one year off being able to drive, and two from being legally able to drink. She can legally have sex. I sometimes think she's far more mature than I am now, let alone how I was at her age. I sincerely hope she doesn't laugh at penis jokes like I do.

16 March 2021

Hubby's had his prick (secret giggling). So have around twenty-three million others. Despite queues and waiting longer than may be sensible during a pandemic, Mr M's very complimentary about the organisation, and about the nurse that administered his dose.

He's been given AstraZeneca. There's been recent blood clotting concerns that resulted in some European countries halting its use. We're not worried, or certainly no more worried than we are about getting deep vein thrombosis (DVT) when we fly. And we used to fly quite a lot.

Why did thoughts of DVT also make me think about Dave Lee Travis? I really don't know how my brain works at times, if it isn't a complete breach of any Trade Description Act to use the words "my brain" and "works" in the same sentence.

Reports continue about the policeman who may have murdered a thirty-three-year-old woman. People are so anxious about their right to roam freely and safely, they are holding outdoor vigils. People are gathering in their hoards to demonstrate about their safety.

That doesn't sound like a safe option in the middle of a pandemic, but even supposed sanctuaries aren't always free from danger. Another Christian leader has posthumously been found guilty of serial sexual abuse.

Most annoying journo strikes again. I shall refer to that journalist as "they", "Layla Keith", or "LK", to disguise the person's sex, hoping it's not offensive to non-binaries about whom this isn't being written. It's about LK whose constant criticising is more predictable, more consistent, and more vexing than our weather.

I've scrolled through thirty-nine screens of LK's reporting, including narrative and graphs. I can find one vaguely positive comment that references the stunning outcome of the vaccine. "So far!" Compliment over. Some might be forgiven if they felt that LK is secretly praying the vaccines will bring horrendous thalidomide-like side effects so they can write about how hasty our government has been to administer doses to every UK adult.

The headline beneath which this fleeting compliment appeared was about the gamble taken with seventeen billions of taxpayers' money. The report criticises the gambles taken when the government didn't tighten restrictions either in a timely manner or with enough severity. It then criticises the so-called vaccine gamble that appears to be one of the most successful roll-outs of our nation's history and of the world.

Where in this diatribe of woe, and reminders of how miserable we should all be, is the balance that impartial journalism is supposed to bring?

I'm no better, am I? I've not written anything complimentary about LK's work. OK, here goes. LK's thirty-nine screens of news followed a well-known technique of delivering good and bad news, commonly called the shit sandwich. Employers use this technique when telling employees about required improvements. The employer starts and ends the discussion talking about tasks the employee has performed well, offering congratulations which surround the matter in respect of which the employee should do better.

Whoops. I've got it the wrong way around. LK's piece isn't a shit sandwich. The good news is in the middle of all the slurry.

I shall resort to saying no more about LK. My mum always told me to say nothing if I hadn't anything kind to say. As with so much of Mum's advice, this is wise. Being bombarded with criticism and negativity damages our well-being. Equally, people can feel better by doing good deeds or by paying compliments, rather than doing or saying the opposite.

Just as I ceased social media activity last August, I shall stop reading articles by LK, which in turn, will stop me moaning about them. I'm trying to read only good news. I'm so tired as I approach a week off work that the weight of any negativity may snap the few remaining threads of my energy, more quickly and easily than a child can shout the word after matching two cards.

Prince Philip has left hospital after a month. News of any ninety-nine-year-old completing a return journey to and from a hospital, is good news.

17 March 2021

I-day

I'm going to the optician.
I realise when I arrive at the car park that it is St Patrick's

day. Leicestershire's hostelries would normally be thronging all day. Conversely, I'm sure I counted more homeless on the streets than shoppers. I haven't any cash on me. I haven't had any for over a year. I feel incredibly guilty walking by, despite long-standing commitments to various charities. I somehow feel donating to registered charities may help the needy more than throwing a few coins at the homeless, akin to standing at the Trevi Fountain. I suspect the three people I pass may disagree. I apologise to each and they seem pleasantly surprised I spoke. Two bid me a lovely day in return. I remind myself I cannot take on their problems.

19 March 2021

I feel like Claudia Winkleman must or Sia, the singer that chooses to mask her face with hair. Why do people choose to impair their vision?

20 March 2021

I have twenty-two bras and two basques.

I have two boobs, excluding any surplus spillage over the top of insufficient cups, or those that have started to grow on my back. I roughly calculate that I wear no more than four of them. I really need to sort that drawer out.

We're enjoying an afternoon tea delivered to our home, a birthday gift for Mr M from his sister and her husband. Hubby is slightly queasy attributing it to vaccine side effects. Of course, it's nothing to do with us propping up the economy until 02:00!

It's the second consecutive day that the previous record of daily vaccines has been beaten. There's been 711,156 in the last twenty-four hours.

It's best we don't have two consecutive nights like the last!

21 March 2021

I was still dozing when I heard "Do you have an NVQ or

equivalent? FFS. I'm fifty-f-ing-seven! How is that relevant?"

I peer out of one eye to see Hubby sitting up staring at his laptop screen. It's census day. Once every decade, our nation answers a few questions to give a picture of all the people and households. This helps make appropriate decisions about funding public services including transport, education, and healthcare.

It seems an odd year to gather this data when excess deaths continue, albeit at reducing rates. We postponed the European Football Championship, known as the Euros, by one year. Why not postpone the census?

22 March 2021

The bra I have been wearing has what looks like a slug on the inside of the left cup. I never even felt it. Ewww!

I'm relieved to realise it is a congealed washing tab. I'm convinced it's less gross because it's from a cleaning product. I still feel gross.

23 March 2021

It's a year since our Prime Minister told us to stay at home, although we'd self-imposed our own lockdown the week before. We didn't wait to be told.

24 March 2021

I've sprayed algae killer on the fence panels which need painting. A gazillion weeds have popped up overnight between bushes and trees. I'm grateful my hair doesn't grow that quickly or I'd resemble Neanderthal woman.

25 March 2021

One of work's executive directors has been asking for lockdown hero nominations. He wants to hear stories of those that reached out to colleagues during times of illness, bereavement, or solitude. I received a message from a friend and colleague that I was her hero. How kind of her to tell me, and the sentiment is reciprocated.

Eighteen of the twenty-one nominations are women. I briefly consider what this bias means, in a department that isn't to my knowledge made up of eighty-five percent females. It could be that women generally reach out more than men. Perhaps women are more likely to take the time to nominate a colleague, and are more likely to nominate another female. I make a note to do the subconscious bias training.

I feel guilty that I feel good about my nomination. Kindness should be prevalent in my opinion. The world would be a better place with more of it from more of us. But why shouldn't it be recognised? I'm in favour of giving credit for a job well done, even if it is that person's job to do whatever deserved the credit. Why not reward behaviour that we should all adopt? Maybe more of us would choose kind in future if it was recognised and rewarded.

26 March 2021

It's the birthday of one of my two best friends, and she's got engaged. With ongoing division across the country, and differences of opinion, and behaviour that prejudices our safe keeping, the announcement of a future union is joyous and welcome.

28 March 2021

My birthday

I remember last year's so clearly. Mr M brought me champagne breakfast in bed and ran me a bath. I finally descended to the kitchen at 14:37 and took a picture of the oven clock as a reminder. I made a birthday cake but couldn't find the candles, so plonked a disproportionately sized Molton Brown one on top. Hubby put a P!nk concert on his laptop while I baked, and friends unexpectedly delivered the ingredients for one of my favourite drinks. We watched Pretty Woman. I remember saying I wouldn't mind doing the same again in 2021.

Mum always said to be careful what I wished for. She is wise. I am not at all happy to be having a second lockdown birthday. I'll have a great day, but it means so many people will continue to be out of work or isolated, in grief, or out of love.

I am happy.

I feel guilty.

I shouldn't.

Leicester Tigers won and my dad seems to be enjoying the union code more than he ever has. I love him and just one of the reasons why, is the effort he makes to take an interest in what others enjoy. He was brought up on rugby league, yet makes the effort to understand rugby union more, so he can enjoy debates and conversations with his son-in law and me.

29 March 2021

My engaged friend came over and we sat outside over lunch.

Only afterwards did I think I must have sounded awkward and looked shifty, rarely making eye contact as I subconsciously searched for a laptop camera hole. Do we need to retrain ourselves how to converse in person?

More footballers are threatening to abandon social media in Thierry Henry's footsteps, in response to the abhorrent abuse he received. Henry said, "The sheer volume of racism, bullying and resulting mental torture to individuals is too toxic to ignore. There HAS to be accountability. It is far too easy to create an account, use it to bully and harass without any consequence. Until this changes, I will be disabling my accounts."

I'm embarrassed to admit that his eloquence and common sense astounded me. He had more than two million Twitter followers.

30 March

I've started to paint the back fence on a glorious day, and an equally stunning bunch of flowers has just arrived from a school friend. We reacquainted a few years ago. She'd seen from my social media post that I was staying near where she lived while I worked in Manchester.

We've kept in touch and I've given her a few things to remind her of our school years. Unfortunately, she doesn't have any possessions from those days, but that's not my story to tell.

I've given her a mug from Boreatton Park, where we spent five days together when we were about twelve. My sister had gone to Switzerland with The Guides. Mum and Dad must have wanted some time alone and so promptly despatched me for a PGL adventure. The acronym comes from the company founder's names, but my friend reminded me over recent drinks that children said it stood for Parents Get Lost.

The adventure cost my parents around fifty pounds I believe, and a lot more in grey hairs when I returned and told the tales of what we'd got up to.

31 March 2021

I'm too stubborn for my own good. I'm on holiday. It's the hottest day of the year and I am painting more fence panels just because I aimed to complete two per day. I have a river running down my back beneath the hazmat suit I bought to wear about a year ago, as a joke during video calls when that joke seemed funny to us.

That suit is ideal for decorating in unless it's twenty-one degrees!

15:05

I am sitting in the sun with a cold glass of white wine like a normal person on a sunny day on holiday.

I've remembered to SORN the car and look forward to the tax refund.

Two azalea plants have just arrived from another school friend for my birthday. I think we were the only two rugby league fans at our school and both support Wigan. Dad followed Wigan as a child, before Wigan reached the top-flight and set numerous records with repeated successes.

My friend's mutual interest in rugby league has been the foundation of our ongoing friendship. We've also found ourselves agreeing about the therapeutic qualities of helping something to grow, which is usually the time our messages get smutty. I did say I laugh at penis jokes.

APRIL 2021

1 April 2021

April fools' day

I will avoid listening to the radio as there's usually a fake news item that the general public is invited to spot. Isn't there enough fake news already?

In actual news, more celebrities are threatening to abandon social media as they recognise the toxicity of the negativity. What happened to the mantra, "If you haven't anything nice to say, don't say anything at all"?

I have finished painting the back fence. Sadly, the one-coat paint lies, so I have added to the job list that I must paint a second coat.

I despise fence painting but love the results. We'll enjoy more time in our garden and need to be thankful of the memories we'll create and keep. I read *Shattered* today. It's the true story of a uni friend who fell forty feet off a roof in 1995, and ended up in a coma with bleeding on the brain. Once out of the coma months later, his parents worked tirelessly to help him talk and walk again. In 2006 when the book was originally published, my friend had recovered to a far greater extent than any medic had believed. He hadn't any long or short-term memory, but he wasn't the cabbage doctors told his parents he would be. Who says cabbage, let alone a medical professional?

I remember when a mutual friend told me about his accident. I remember sprinting off the uni nightclub dancefloor to Leicester Royal Infirmary. I remember one of the first people I saw was also a uni friend who was studying medicine. I remember being half drunk but rapidly sobering up, being scared and shocked. I remember arriving at his bed by which his parents sat, whom I met for the first time. They're not memories anyone would wish to have. But I need to cherish the fact that I can remember.

3 April 2021

I'm almost too embarrassed to tell Hubby how long it has been since I last washed our bedsheets.

I've done three loads of washing including the bed covers and wondered how it's possible for two adults living in lounge wear to create so much laundry, despite insufficiently frequent bed linen changes.

Hubby offered to make the bed while I cook dinner. He's been at it for forty minutes and dinner is ready. What is he doing up there?

Apparently, he'd made the bed once, but realised the duvet was in the cover perpendicular to how it should have been, so started again. I consider this may be a ploy so that I don't ever ask him to make the bed again. I must stay strong!

4 April 2021

It's the birthday of a friend who lives in South Africa. Last year's card to him left Guernsey on 23 March and arrived at his around seven months later, in October. I sent this year's card last November, and it still hasn't arrived.

Hubby's built the new barbecue. We have succumbed to gas in what we previously felt was a regressive step away from tradition. What I hope it will be, is a step closer to having barbecues. We won't object to using gas even when it's just the two of us. Our previous barbecue needed a bag of coal that cost eight pounds. It took forty minutes to get anywhere near hot enough to cook anything other than toast, during which time, our spontaneity would crumble to dust, resembling the bottom of the barbecue which would take me thirty minutes to sweep. That is until Hubby told me there was a trap door that releases the ashes in less than the three minutes it took us to eat our burgers.

After numerous hours, Mr M has successfully constructed the three burner contraption, and has promptly hidden it under the made-to-measure cover. That cover cost an astronomical three figures, just so the barbecue fits snugly enough that the slightest breeze won't dislodge it, and send it down the lane to the sheltered houses. Our barbecue is in its own sheltered accommodation.

We are determined to spend more time in our garden, especially as it is so much more aesthetically pleasing after all the hours spent painting the fences.

5 April 2021

It's six degrees and I am sitting outside admiring the garden fences and sheltered barbecue. I won't absorb any natural vitamin D as every inch of my skin is covered, apart from a few millimetres around my eyes above my snood which protects me from nineteen-mile-per-hour winds.

I cannot imagine how ridiculous I looked when my sister video called from a local park she was visiting to meet our folks.

When they're together is the only chance I get to see my folks, since Mum's mobile is a brick that should be thrown in a pond. But that would be littering, and in a few years' time it may be worth three figures, like my old Nokia 3210 that I discarded a week before reading of its antique value.

6 April 2021

It's snowing!

7 April 2021

It's my second day back at work and I already feel shattered. All I am doing is sitting at my desk, yet I feel more drained than a wet lettuce whizzed round an electric colander.

I'm not expending energy gambolling between the living room and kitchen like a spring lamb that isn't lost but can't go anywhere. I'm not painting fences in twenty-degree heat.

I'm sitting on what Hubby describes as my spreading backside. It's a description surely only used by those secure enough in their relationship to know that its audible use will not invoke a decree nisi.

But how does anyone work until they are of pensionable age? If lockdown has shown me anything, it is that I will not be bored or at a loose end when I retire.

8 April 2021

The paper for the feature wall in the blue room, the second spare bedroom that is used more rarely than a condom by a nun, has arrived.

Why do I keep adding to the list of jobs to do? It's not as if there isn't plenty on there, or that the blue room is hideous. Admittedly, it's a little beige and needs some colour. But it's nothing that some new bedding wouldn't achieve more cheaply and more quickly, assuming I don't leave it up to SB to put the duvet cover on.

I have also today received a refund for a comedy event that was postponed from last May until February this year, and then cancelled. When I didn't get any further correspondence following the event's cancellation, I wrote asking for a refund. I sent around a dozen emails politely requesting my money back. I received the same promise of a refund each time, with increased tales of woe about furloughed staff and cancelled bank accounts, lost puppies* and drowning bunnies*.

(* not strictly true).

I'm a big believer that no one gets different results adopting the same approach, so I tried a different tactic.

Within hours, the money I was owed was in my account. This is miraculous given I was repeatedly told all the company's payment systems had been closed. Simples, as the meerkats say.

If I calculate an hourly wage based on the time spent to recover my debt, I should be self-reporting for not paying myself the minimum wage. But it's the principle. I paid for something I didn't receive. I'm entitled to a refund.

I got Just the Tonic I needed by way of a refund, and shall attend future events when able.

9 April 2021

Prince Philip's died two months before his one-hundredth birthday.

Nikki Grahame, former contestant on *Big Brother* and TV personality has died aged thirty-eight. She'd suffered anorexia for three decades. At the same age as her illness started, Prince Philip was abruptly separated from his parents and four elder sisters with whom he'd never share a home again.

Nikki suffered for three decades before a premature death while Prince Philip became the longest serving consort. He was two months short of potentially receiving two birthday cards from his wife.

Both had some privileges I will never be afforded. They've both also had experiences I wouldn't want, and with which I may not have coped. Sadly, in the end, Nikki couldn't cope.

Meanwhile Kate Garraway's husband is home after spending a year in hospital with Covid. They'll have to learn to adjust and cope with the ongoing effects while his prognosis remains uncertain. For now, I'm sure they're all grateful to have him home.

10 April 2021

A female jockey rode The Grand National winner, Minella Times. Or, in other words, a jockey rode The Grand National winner, Minella Times.

It reminds me of when Andy Murray corrected a journalist

who wrongly stated Sam Querrey was the first US player to reach a major semi-final since 2009.

"Male player!" corrected Murray, because Serena Williams had won twelve Grand Slam tournaments since 2009.

He was right to correct that journalist. But should we be focussing on the gender of The National's jockey? Doesn't this just continue to fuel the division and any sexism that remains?

It certainly draws attention to it. It promotes discussion. It raises awareness, which can encourage change.

Would women have been partly enfranchised in 1918 and more broadly in 1928 if it wasn't for the suffrage movement championing the cause?

Would civil partnerships for same-sex couples have come into effect from 5 December 2005 without the lobbyists?

Would 2020 have seen five percent of FTSE 100 companies led by women, if they hadn't fought for a boardroom place?

Would companies be trying to redress the imbalances amongst the demography of their employees, if awareness of the supposed bias wasn't continually mooted?

How far should we go? I'm a childless woman who's been married three years, although Mr M and I will celebrate a decade together this June. Prior to meeting SB, I wasn't steadily dating and didn't have childcare duties. I have seen and still see the benefits of both sexes being able to work. Conversely, I think it's also made many house prices unaffordable for those with a single income.

I know some who spit, (not literally, especially not during a pandemic), at the assumption that equal rights should be given to those who haven't delivered equal contributions. I've worked more than my share of fifteen-hour days and weekends, and studied for qualifications. As a salaried employee, my average hourly earnings were often far lower than those of colleagues who worked to rule. But I've been promoted at what I think were roughly the right times in the circumstances. I don't feel I was overlooked in favour of male colleagues.

I feel we should be focussing on making it possible for the

right person to be in the right job, even if they face hindrances. It shouldn't matter whether they're male, female, transgender, non-binary, questioning, disabled, (physically or mentally), lesbian, gay, or bisexual, a parent or not. Shouldn't the sole factor be whether they can perform the role?

Organisations spend huge amounts striving to achieve some arbitrary percentages in a potentially biased attempt to demonstrate a lack of bias. Target percentages can result in people being promoted, despite a lack of capability, just so an employer can tick a box.

Shouldn't we be spending the money making roles accessible to those that could deliver them, if it wasn't for a hurdle which isn't their fault they have to jump, and shouldn't have to?

My first employer recruited an external consultant to review why women in their thirties were leaving the firm for reasons other than childbirth. I was invited to join one of the several groups gathered to discuss the same. Each group was as diverse as possible, represented by different disciplines, different grades and sexes of staff and partners.

After the usual introductions as if at an AA meeting, (not that I'd know), we proceeded with the discussion. One lady in her thirties said she was contemplating leaving as she was being overlooked for promotion in favour of colleagues in the same department, who'd joined on the same date she had.

Never one to be shy to raise a hand, I asked her to remind us of her working history that she'd alluded to in her intro, and to tell us about her promoted peers. She'd been part-time for two years to collect and drop off children at school. Great. My employer was being flexible. Tick. We needed that.

In the previous two years, she'd not done any overtime on top of her part-time work. Her promoted peers worked full-time, on top of which they regularly worked additional and unpaid hours. I mentally calculated that her promoted peers had around two years more experience than she had, despite having started their career at the same time.

I asked her if she'd considered the reason she wasn't being

promoted, may be because she had less experience, wasn't ready for promotion and may not cope. Thankfully she wasn't Medusa, or I wouldn't be here to write the tale.

During our group's coffee break, every man thanked me for saying what they had wanted to, but had feared they'd be accused of sexism if they had. Could it be as wrong as sexism that they didn't feel able to ask the question I had asked?

As crucial as it is not to be positively prejudicial, why shouldn't we celebrate successes? Surely we shouldn't shy away from being proud of those achievements that have been reached in the face of additional adversity.

Rachael Blackmore jumped sixteen fences in The National. She'll have jumped a heck of a lot more hurdles than that to be a successful jockey.

If a career as a jockey is going to become as commonplace amongst women as it is amongst men, we need to celebrate women's victories. It's non-sensical that the typically slighter-framed sex, arguably more suited to the career, is almost as rare as rocking horse poo.

I will celebrate success. I will be loud and proud that a female jockey rode The National's winner. Well done Rachael. I don't seek to belittle previous male victors, or future male winners. You're all winners.

11 April 2021

It's like someone's punctured a bean bag in the sky as poly-styrene-like hail falls mid-way through my second coat of paint on the fence.

Within minutes the sun has come out. The changes in weather mirror the roller coaster of emotions so many of us are experiencing. Isn't it proven that our mood is directly correlated to the weather? I must take my vitamin D tablet.

12 April 2021

They've only gone and done it. The nine most vulnerable groups have all had their first Covid vaccine, three days ahead of Thursday's target. That's about thirty-two million people. I'm in the next group.

13 April 2021

I've booked both vaccines, and the first is on Thursday.

14 April 2021

I know someone who was supposed to listen to a webinar about work-life blend. Apparently, it's not called work-life balance, anymore. Ironically she felt she had too much work to be able to take an hour to listen.

15 April 2021

11:25

While waiting to be jabbed, I heard much giggling about little prick jokes, which the staff must have heard incessantly, but still seemed to appreciate. The entire process was slicker than an oil spill, including Hubby's chauffeuring service, as I refused to tax my car.

It was surprisingly pleasant to be out, not least as the pharmacist speedily dismissed reports that I should avoid alcohol for two weeks. The pubs have just opened for goodness' sake. I don't need such negativity, and publicans' tills don't either. Telling me I can't have a glass of wine for two weeks is about as well received as the news in Ireland that they were the first to trial the smoking ban in pubs.

The pharmacist equally quickly glossed over the pre-prepared spiel to dispel any blood clotting concerns I may have had. I told him I was more likely to be run over by a bus.

20:00

It's nine hours since my vaccine and I feel fine. Phew. From what I've heard, those with side effects usually start to feel them after around eight hours.

21:00

I am colder than my usual lizard-like self. I have goose bumps on goose bumps and am turning a colour with which Hubby's navarra blue Audi cannot compete. Bedtime.

16 April 2021

I feel like I have been run over by a bus.

It hurts to open my eyelids. Even my little toe aches. How am I supposed to spend all day typing when it feels like my fingers may snap at the joints if I dare to bend them?

"Take the day off," says Mr M rather sensibly. I ignored him as I wanted to finish a report before next week which is fully booked with meetings.

16:30

I've finished the report and am diving into a bath to soak my aching joints.

17 April 2021

It's the day of Prince Philip's funeral. Current restrictions mean his wife of seventy-three years, Her Majesty the Queen, will sit on her own in the chapel, the twenty-nine other guests all socially distanced from each other.

I wonder if this more intimate ceremony is what the royal family should always be allowed.

Hubby watched a few minutes before announcing "No one

does it better!" He meant the British people are the best at ceremonial events. Precise. Dignified. He's right.

People at work say practice makes perfect. It's perfect practice that makes perfect. Today will have been rehearsed until it couldn't be done other than perfectly. There was even a spare hearse in case of breakdown.

RIP Prince Philip.

18 April 2021

I feel fully recovered from my side effects. I've no hesitation about going for the second vaccine. It's the next stage of a large step to freedom. But it's sobering to read that new cases per week globally have nearly doubled in the last two months. I'm sure testing has increased which impacts on the stats.

But anyone that thinks we can fling our masks while cheering for our freedom, needs to dial down the Emmeline Pankhurst bra-burning emulation. Otherwise we may find the only thing burning is the bridge to complete freedom that might not hold long enough to get there.

Hark at me. I could be a successful journalist with this negativity. I must have been reading too much yesterday. I was sitting in Tit Corner reading the headlines, pointing out to Hubby that even news that could have been positive, had the opposite spin. I admit there's not much joy to be found amongst funerals and death. But Chelsea's win over Man City came with a headline focussing on Man City's failure to be able to achieve a quadruple of major titles. It focussed on Chelsea ending Man City's hopes. But Chelsea have hopes. Chelsea may win the FA Cup.

I hope not. I'd like Leicester City to beat Southampton this evening in the other semi, and go on to win. I'm glad it doesn't clash with the rugby union match between Leicester Tigers and Bath this afternoon.

I don't know why it reminds me of a trip to Jersey that my mum, my sister, and I took a few years ago. I'd booked it all and met Sister and Mum at Ringway, (as I still call Manchester airport). We were enjoying pre-flight drinks when Mum decided she fancied a cigarette. I told her where the outdoor smoking area was. I added that the terminal from which we were departing was the only one at the airport that had a smoking area, and I'd contacted the airline to ask if our flight could depart from it.

"Oh, thank you sweetie pie. You are so thoughtful."

19 April 2021

I feel right as rain, typically after the weekend and in time for work. That phrase was first recorded in 1894. The simile allusion is unclear, but seems to me as ridiculous as announcing I'm fit as a fiddle. What has the shapely stringed instrument got to do with fitness?

It's a ridiculous statement for me to make anyway. If I honestly answered any question about my well-being, no one would think I was fit as a fiddle. If I was a racehorse, I'd probably be put down.

I wear glasses.

I get a nosebleed from my left nostril at least once a month.

Both ears ring incessantly with tinnitus and my left hurts when I yawn. I have water behind it causing unexpected and excruciating stabbing pains. The doctor told me three years ago the water would dissipate after a few months.

My left arm creaks at the shoulder when I make circular motions. I tore a muscle when I tripped over fresh air at Paddington Station eighteen months ago. I nosedived only slightly less elegantly than Greg Luganis in the 1988 Seoul Olympics when he hit his head on the diving board. Instinctively, as I flew through the station air for what seemed like several minutes, I extended my left arm to stop my nose being the first part of my anatomy to break my fall, and tore the shoulder muscle in the process. But I carried on my journey and gave my presentation to a few hundred attendees, with my arm duly elevated in a makeshift sling, using my scarf. I didn't discover the tear for a few weeks after I eventually conceded to the pain, and dragged my-self to a physio. He told me the muscle was now entirely knotted and needed painful manipulation to help a proper recovery. Joy. I never learn.

My left thumb carpometacarpal joint aches in cold weather, ever since I partially tore the ligament when I fell over walking from a car park to my employer's office. (I spot a theme. I'd not even been drinking). It was my first day after a three-week holiday to watch The Ashes in Australia. My employer's own doctor signed me off for four weeks despite my insistence I could work.

The base of my back at the right, just above my cheek, oc-casionally hurts so badly I cannot sit down. This pain can shoot down my leg, which, in positive news that I celebrate with wine, convinces me it's not kidney related.

My right knee occasionally spasms. I feel like I might im-personate a tumbling Jenga tower. At one moment I can look stable and be upright, but can collapse quicker than the current plans for a football European Super League, with even less warn-ing.

I don't know how I broke my ankles, as I never had them x-rayed at the time. Both my ankles suffer now if I wear flats for any length of time, or if I kneel up with my buttocks resting on them. It's hugely ironic that my broken ankles are more comfort-able in heels, as my parents never let me wear heels until I was sixteen, concerned I may damage the immature bones.

X-rays taken following other accidents revealed the exist-ing breaks. One doctor told me he could heal one of them, by re-breaking my ankle. That was six weeks before I was due to start uni, and I would have been in plaster for eighteen weeks.

"Jog on, doc!" was as polite as I could be.

I remember various sporting accidents that may have caused the breaks. But it's bizarre that on the occasions I have thought I may have done so and have been to A & E, I've only sprained them. I've got two pairs of crutches in the garage, one from Italy and one from Australia. I purchased the latter when I fell into a friend's wedding venue and then couldn't stand up. My foot was perpendicular to my leg and several guests were telling me I'd broken my ankle and I needed to go to hospital. I'd flown twelve thousand miles, taking over a day, to be able to attend a wedding that would last twenty minutes. I wasn't going to be able to do a return hospital journey in that time, and wasn't about to miss the ceremony, or ruin it for the kind guests offering to accompany me to hospital. Eventually at 23:00 I decided I needed to go, as the strap on my Prada heel had started to dig in the swelling so much, my foot looked like a size twenty-two person wearing a size twelve pair of leggings.

On sight of it, still at a right-angle to my leg that would have avoided any requirement for a set square at school, I was told I'd broken it. The radiographer took x-rays to determine the exact location and extent of the break.

Three doctors looked at my x-rays, as the first and second couldn't believe that my ankle wasn't broken after all. I was thrilled, until they told me it wasn't such good news. Not only would they not plaster it, but initially, and perhaps understandably, the medics weren't prepared to loan me any crutches. They were concerned by my attempts to numb the pain with alcohol as the wedding venue didn't have any painkillers. They thought that alcohol, combined with crutching around Sydney, was a cocktail that would end up in another visit to the hospital.

I showed the staff how well I could cope on crutches as I raced up and down the corridor, after a disproportionate length of time arguing that under no circumstances was I removing my other Prada to do so.

On that display, they had to agree to lend me some walking aids. "Bring them back tomorrow, and we will return your forty-dollar deposit." I used those crutches for four weeks, by which time I'd returned to the UK, and they sit in our garage to this day.

But who wants to hear my list of (mostly) self-inflicted injuries when they ask how I am? When anyone asks how I am, instead of saying I'm right as rain, it would be more accurate to say I'm a shower of sh*t.

20 April 2021

Football fans, clubs that aren't involved, and pundits are vociferous in their opposition to any Super League. Our PM has said nothing is off the table to block it. The minds behind the Super League claim intervention to block it would prevent competition. What's less competitive than a league without promotion or relegation?

21 April 2021

Her Majesty the Queen's ninety-fifth birthday

Our Monarch is still mourning the death of her husband. Is a day spent mourning better than the alternative of not having the day?

Mr M spontaneously suggested a bottle of fizz, as if the grown up association of it counters the almost child-like dinner of fish fingers, chips, and baked beans. The food felt like more of a treat, possibly because of the associated memories. Mum would cook fish fingers before the Brownies, and as I got older, before the Guides. We continued the fish finger theme every Friday, before I was old enough to go to pubs (or old enough to be allowed, at least). Fish finger teas (it's not dinner, up North), have been with me my entire solid food life. They've lasted longer than boyfriends, favourite dolls, snuggly jumpers, or most adored shoes. Fish fingers are a foundation of my life. And I shall drink fizz as I eat them.

22 April 2021

Wigan beat Castleford 22-12 in the rugby league. Leicester City beat West Brom 3-0. I am also beat. By what, I don't know.

23 April 2021

A friend I met on cricket holiday wished me happy Saint George's Day. I was embarrassed I hadn't even realised, especially as I had known when it was Saint Patrick's Day. I don't know why the English don't celebrate like the Irish. We celebrate Saint Patrick's Day more vigorously than our own Saint's Day. It doesn't make any sense to me. Maybe it's because our Saint was Greek and as far as anyone can tell, never stepped foot on England's green and pleasant land.

Hubby's returned from golf to an email confirming he's accredited as a financial ombudsman. He can send his complaint decisions without any review.

We celebrated al fresco with our neighbours and wine. It got too late to cook the fajitas so we propped up the economy a bit more with a chip-shop dash. All the excitement and fresh air must have worn me out, as I was too tired to drink more wine and retired to bed by 21:00.

24 April 2021

Every day is a school day. I have learnt that sausages do not grill when the cooker is set to top oven heating.

I've been trawling photos to select some for my parents' golden wedding anniversary card. I'd forgotten so many of the happy occasions I snapped. I ended up roaring with laughter at a photo of a uni friend and I dressed as cleaners to go to a fancy dress party.

I was in my fourth year at uni and rented a room in a large house that the uni bought and converted. There were about twenty-seven rooms and a few kitchens and bathrooms. I'd first seen what became my room, when I'd flown back from France, for a friend's twenty-first. She occupied the room then, and as soon as I saw it, I decided I'd apply to have it the following year. Fourth year students, especially those who'd been abroad the previous year, got priority. The uni recognised it was almost impossible in those days, for students living abroad, to find a room in a house in the UK to rent from a private landlord the following academic year.

I loved living there. Most of us had to make new friends in our final year, as the majority of those with whom we'd started uni, had graduated after three years, leaving us to a final fourth year without them.

On the night of the fancy dress party, two of us acquired cleaners' outfits. We donned lurid eye shadow and tan tights, and didn't stop laughing all night.

While choosing photos, our decorator has hung the wallpaper chosen for the feature walls in the two spare bedrooms. Neither room needed a refurb, but the blue room has always been a bit beige and we'd got a bit bored of the yellow walls in the green room.

25 April 2021

I surprised myself at how excited I became looking at paint pots and brush cleaner in the DIY store. I normally only experience this when looking at shoes, handbags or makeup and facial products. But I suppose paint is makeup for walls.

Hubby wasn't surprised that I wore heels, but still thought I looked ridiculous.

"You're the only person I know to wear stilettoes to buy paint!"

I was desperate to spot someone else with talons on their feet. There must be others who've bought shoes, clothes and handbags in various sales using the refunds from cancelled holidays. Surely, I'm not the only one who's done so and not been able to wear the purchases since, and will take any opportunity to do so?

I love how tall I feel wearing my four-inch heels, and not just physically. But my calf and other muscles need to get used to my feet being in something other than slippers. I may look ridiculous, but if I'm going out with Hubby, I'm doing so with nothing less than eight inches.

I started reading the paper when we got home. It usually takes me all week to read some of it, but I enjoy it more than any social media trawling I used to waste time doing. I've read more books, mainly memoirs, than ever before, and still have time for a broadsheet on Sundays.

Unfortunately, Mr M and I realised after an evening video call with mates, that we'd not communicated with each other. Neither of us defrosted the mince for tonight's meal, and so we decided to prop up the economy and pick up a takeaway instead.

26 April 2021

It's Monday.

27 April 2021

Hubby's fasting today while I enjoy the leftover Indian. The flavours take me back to my first and only trip to India in 2005. It saddens me to think of the deepening pandemic crisis there. I've said for months it's pointless UK residents being vaccinated and safe if the rest of the world isn't.

There's been over forty-seven million vaccines in the UK, of which almost thirty-four million are first doses. Compared to some countries, the UK is bingeing on jabs.

Hubby and I have binged almost six series of *Line of Duty*. We don't normally follow a crowd, but couldn't resist the police drama about internal corruption any longer. It recently attracted around eleven million viewers, about the same as watched Prince Philip's funeral.

The last episode of series six is on Sunday. We've been rationing the episodes so we don't have to wait a week in between each. Thankfully this is not the same as wartime rations. We're so privileged to have on-demand TV, we've lost what little patience we (read, I) had. We (I) want it all. Now.

I try to persuade myself that I am not impatient or unreasonable, and attribute my behaviour to the menopause. My brain can't remember the characters if I only watch one episode per week. I'd end up asking Mr M who people were, what they were doing and why, and what was going on. I'd have to ask what day of the week it was, if it wasn't obviously Sunday, given that's the day of broadcast.

We avoided one cliff edge by watching two episodes consecutively, including the penultimate one of what may be the final series. I was reminded of a Victoria Wood sketch in which she asks shoppers' opinions in a street survey. Her clipboard notes prompt her to break the ice with a joke. She tells one passer-by two jokes, and is immediately concerned she's a joke short for the next person. Comedy genius. But we're definitely short of an episode to watch tomorrow.

28 April 2021

I am hearing things, other than the ringing that tinnitus brings. I could have sworn I heard a cork pop in the kitchen as I finished working in the study.

I sprinted into the kitchen in a display of exercise not seen since before 16 March 2020, to be as quickly disappointed by the lack of open wine.

I gave Mr M a frosty glare that mirrored the overnight forecast. Apparently April's had five times as much frost as usual, and has been exceptionally dry.

Well, I can vouch for the latter. It's wine Wednesday and Hubby's not even popped a cork.

29 April 2021

Hubby has started to sing before I am out of bed. I always struggle to stir. I usually slowly lift one eyelid at a time, as if each was weighed down by bricks. But it means that we're not clambering for the shower at the same time, and so Hubby is always dressed before me. Perhaps a gentle serenade is just what I need to be enticed out of bed.

Except, there's nothing gentle about Mr M singing about his ablutions to the tune of a former teabag advert. His dulcet tones ring louder than my tinnitus, as he crabs around the bedroom while singing, simultaneously crossing then uncrossing his arms in front of his torso.

I pull the cover back over my head.

30 April 2021

15:00

Football clubs, players and associated organisations are switching off tw*tter, insta-whatsit, and stalk-book until 23:59 on Monday. It's in response to the discriminatory online abuse of players and others connected to the sport. It may sufficiently dent their advertising income so they have to consider how they can help stop such trolling. I have abandoned social media, but it has a place and can be beneficial if not abused.

We have a sporting clash tonight. Thankfully, we can record one and watch it later, as if we'd requested a change in start time.

Pascal Gaüzère is the rugby referee. He has the physique of Mr Bean and if his last game is anything to go by, equally weak eyesight, according to some.

Tonight, he sent the Tigers' captain to the sin-bin, prompting our replacement captain to ask if he could talk to the rest of the team.

"You won't start the game, will you?" quipped one of the commentators. It was a jibe that assumed the listeners had seen an incident in the Six Nations, when Mr ~~Bean~~ Gaüzère didn't afford such time in a similar scenario. The opposing team scored while the England team was huddling to discuss its defence strategy.

May 2021

1 May 2021

I have painted the green room. It didn't need decorating. I loved the yellow walls adorned with gilt-framed Klimt prints of *The Kiss* and *Danae.* I love my wedding dress displayed on a mannequin, as Hubby suggested.

We decided to have a feature wall papered, and in doing so, needed to paint the rest. It's not a job I like. It's tedious, messy, smelly, laborious, and boring. Some think it should be a blue job (and probably would be if we hadn't burned our bras in sexism protest).

I can't deny I'm always thrilled at the results. I was determined today to revel in the delights of home ownership. I was intent on being thankful to have a green room to paint. I purposefully tried to appreciate the time I had to myself while adorning the walls with their own makeup.

It didn't work. I don't care how many webinars I watch, or articles I read about the well-being benefits of being thankful. I tried, really hard, and I still hate painting.

I opened my post which included a card from Her Majesty, the Queen, thanking me for the sympathy card I sent. I thought about returning thanks, but then realised the mutual appreciation has to have a final word, and it's probably fitting that Her Majesty has it, even if she did send it second class.

2 May 2021

I am so stiff, but am determined to put the spare room back together. Having decided to have a feature wall, we've also decided to replace all sockets with stainless steel ones.

Annoyingly, some of those we need aren't available for collection today. I am hugely frustrated. We decided what we wanted, and I clicked. I wanted Hubby to collect them, today. We have to wait two whole days.

Patience, Mrs M. But herein starts the simmering of panic that may boil over. I worry that we haven't done a job that would have been perfect for a wet weekend. It's been postponed until a time when we hope the sun will have more than one hat on, and we won't want to stay indoors a second longer. I worry that I'll sit soaking up the vitamin D thinking of the indoor chores mounting up, until they become so numerous, that my stress level at having too much to do becomes its own chore to manage.

Why did we even agree to decorate a perfectly beautiful room, given the stress it incites?

Why am I reading three books when I struggle to cope with having too much to do?

Why am I panicking about any of it? It's not like I have to manage a vaccine roll-out. I'm not a doctor working round the clock as they are in India.

Why am I comparing? My concerns are my concerns. They are real. They are valid.

3 May 2021

It's Northern Ireland's one-hundredth birthday. Hubby's made cookies, and although not for that reason, they still feel like a birthday treat.

Last year, like so many, we baked when flour supplies permitted. We spent Sundays preparing for, cooking, and eating lunch.

Yesterday's venison went untouched. Mr M was too out of sorts by the news his golf club's nineteenth hole burnt down on Saturday evening. Nine fire crews spent five hours putting out the blaze that demolished a building, as I sat safely at home, patting myself about my decorating prowess.

Thankfully, no one was hurt in the fire. The investigation has begun, and I cooked fish fingers, chips, and beans. We ate them watching the World Snooker Cup final. It's momentous. It's the first sporting event in around fourteen months to be in front of a full crowd. The Crucible Theatre, where it's held, is named after a container in which metals may be melted. It pays homage to Sheffield, the centre of Britain's steelmaking, following the innovation in the eighteenth century.

It hosts nine hundred and eighty spectators today. One thousand, nine hundred and sixty eyes focus on the oblong table that is almost twelve feet by six, with six pockets into which players attempt to roll the balls, across the green baize.

There isn't a mouth in sight. They're all hidden behind cloth that covers the facial pockets. But it's still obvious everyone is smiling. Every attendee applauds as the players emerge.

But this applause is different to any other snooker match or final. This applause doesn't just recognise the achievements of, and encourage, the two finalists. It thanks those who've enabled this occasion to have a live and full audience. It tells every nurse, doctor, hospital porter, virologist, rule-abiding citizen, event organiser, official, player and family member, that the audience is grateful.

Sheffield applauds you all.

A nation applauds you all. We may not be standing on our doorsteps clapping the NHS at 20:00 on Thursdays anymore. But from our sofas on a wet bank holiday, this annual final gives us a reason to remain glued to the box. This is a historical occasion, as any final always is. But this final is taking place in unprecedented times.

Mr M and I have an added interest, as Leicester's Mark Selby, the Jester, is a finalist alongside Shaun Murphy. Shaun left England to live in Dublin from where his wife comes. I suspect he won't be distracted by the division of Ireland a century ago.

6 May 2021

There are sixty French vessels off St Helier as the country's fishermen protest over Brexit rights.

Jersey is the largest of the Channel Islands. It's a Crown dependency, and although not technically part of the UK, it is defended by it. The UK is sending the navy.

If history is anything to go by, the French will have surrendered by the weekend.

7 May 2021

I can barely contain my lack of shock, horror, and surprise. The French have retreated. The fire at Hubby's golf course was arson. Marks & Spencer still thinks Aldi customers may mistakenly think they are purchasing an M&S caterpillar cake when they're in an Aldi store.

Seriously? We're expected to believe that a shopper that enters a clearly labelled Aldi store, and places an Aldi packaged cake that is named Cuthbert (and not Colin, like the M&S version), into an Aldi labelled receptacle, may somehow be confused?

Even if any of that was believable, the Grand Prix speed with which customers are jettisoned through the Aldi checkout, is surely sufficient evidence one is not in any M&S store.

But the possibly tenuous claim by M&S has created lots of publicity for both, and probably lots more money for some lawyers.

8 May 2021

The hat-trick. Wigan lost in the Challenge Cup after yesterday's defeats by Leicester teams in football and rugby union.

9 May 2021

My folks' golden wedding anniversary. I can't be there because of the rule of six.

Our neighbour invited SB to join him in the garden for a cigar at 11:30. His partner and I joined shortly after. It wasn't too much longer, when we all decided some fizz was in order, to remotely celebrate my folks' achievement.

By around 15:30, the recycling was feeling well and truly loved, but our stomachs weren't. After a brief sandwich interlude, the four of us reconvened.

By 18:30, my neck was burnt. I'd stupidly never thought to apply sun cream, in temperatures that were well below average for the time of year. Our skin isn't used to being exposed, another previously unconsidered consequence of the pandemic. Alongside the concerns we may face increased numbers of eating disorders and other mental illnesses, we may face increased cases of skin cancer.

10 May 2021

It's mental health awareness week. I'd like to think I am aware of people's mental well-being every week, and am certainly aware that others are not.

12 May 2021

There's an article in the Sunday Times that Gwyneth Paltrow (GP) has been drinking every night and eating carbs!

She's imbibed two drinks per night, and the article leads us to believe that some contained whiskey. They definitely contained quinoa.

"Who drinks multiple drinks, seven nights a week? That's not healthy."

Well, GP, it shouldn't take more than a quick glance at the obesity crises in your country and in ours, and at the rising rates of diabetes and alcohol dependency, together with related crime incidents, to answer your question. Lots of people drink far too much, all the time.

Perhaps you should be asking why they don't drink quinoa. It's probably because most of us can't even pronounce it. So when we try to ask the supermarket staff for its location, we end up asking for wine.

That could be my excuse next time anyone asks why we buy so much wine.

"Couldn't pronounce quinoa!"

GP shares rituals with us mere planet germs, that suggest she is more deeply cleansed than a sanitising wipe that's been drenched in disinfectant. Her initials mimic those that help cure the sick, and even she resorted to double shots and pasta over the last year.

The rest of us should be comforted that our numerous bottles of wine, and takeaways each week, are comparatively proportionate.

But for my own sanity, I add GP to the list of people whose quotes and articles I will avoid in future. She's in great company with Layla Keith.

Nevertheless, I decide to skip wine tonight.

13 May 2021

The plumbers have arrived to fit the new boiler. We're without central heating and hot water until tomorrow evening.

I hadn't expected that to be an issue in mid-May but it's barely ten degrees outside, and so I have donned more layers than a mille-feuille.

We're blessed to have a gas fire in the living room and a portable oil heater. I also contemplated putting both ovens on and leaving their doors open.

If only I still lived with Mum and Dad in Blackburn. They've got around forty-three blankets that haven't been used since duvets became affordable to them, around forty-three years ago. If only their blankets could smother the spread of the virus.

The case numbers in Blackburn are three times the national average. I'm trying not to think about future eventualities, although our PM isn't ruling out any action.

We'll abide by the rules at the time, but I hope, and not just for us, that my parents can come to stay in a fortnight.

A great friend sent me a complimentary email. A psychic couldn't have timed it better. Her words lifted my dampened spirits. Shouldn't we all do what we can to make kindness more transmissible than any virus?

14 May 2021

We have a new boiler. The plumbers and electrician spent two hours trying to understand why it wouldn't turn off. Apparently, there's a manual override that was activated, resulting in it being on permanently. I felt relieved that I'm not alone when I overlook the seemingly obvious.

The new thermostat will apparently learn and remember our behaviour and heating preferences. Sometimes, I can't remember my own name!

15 May 2021

Today's haircut, my first since last year, has lifted my mood. If only it lifted a proportionate amount of weight!

Hubby took me into town afterwards, as we both needed watch batteries.

I bought a watch with diamonds on its face. Apparently, it's traditional to give diamonds on the tenth wedding anniversary. Mr M and I have been together ten years next month, so that's good enough for me. But I knew better than to suggest he should buy it for me.

I didn't feel well when we got home, so decided to take a nap. I woke to see the second half of the Tigers' match against Harlequins. Tigers had two players sin-binned. I often say that good discipline may not win a game, but poor discipline can cost it. Thankfully, we still won, although we had to wait to find out. We had to wait as we didn't watch the second half live. We recorded it so we could watch the build up to the one hundred and fortieth FA Cup final.

Chelsea have won it eight times and been in fifteen finals. Leicester haven't won any of its previous four finals.

The fans seemed to make as much noise as if Wembley was at capacity, despite it being only one-quarter full. It's the largest crowd of the government's pilot events. It's probably required as many hours to organise as it would for eighty thousand fans. All attendees have been sent tests, and must return a negative result to be able to attend.

As has become the norm, the Leicester owners wrote to each season-ticket holder, enclosing memorabilia to help the recipient support the team, whether attending or not. It certainly seemed as though Leicester's fans were the loudest. And they were duly rewarded with a narrow one-nil victory, but only after Chelsea had a goal disallowed for offside. There'll be continued discussions about the merits of the Video Assistant Referee, but the Leicester fans today were most definitely in favour of it.

The win is as welcome as the news that there's less than one thousand people in hospital with the virus, and the average daily deaths is in single digits.

But there are pockets of concern. Our PM has asked residents in various hot spots to be sensible. Last time he suggested that, we had a national lockdown a week later. Some think we've already demonstrated we can't be trusted to be sensible, and need specific instruction.

Nevertheless, I hope he doesn't invoke another lockdown, as my folks are coming in less than two weeks, and we haven't had a meal together as a family since January 2020.

16 May 2021

The rain's been interrupted so after a zoom call with some neighbours about a proposed housing development, I do the weeding. It's not kind to my joints, and I am thankful that I finish just before the drops fall.

A friend has invited me to dinner next week. We've been discussing this for some time, and now I am consumed with fear about going out. I start contemplating what excuses I can give. I even consider saying I have symptoms and so must isolate. But that would be a lie. I like my friend. I like food. Why would I try to excuse myself and stay home, when I've done nothing but stay home for the last fifteen months? It seems this pandemic has turned me into an antisocial, intolerant, greying misery.

17 May 2021

I have psyched myself up for dinner.

While getting ready, I try to reach a handbag from the shelf that sits above the wardrobe rail. Eventually, I put down my phone and use both hands. I remind myself to be thankful to have both arms and that I should use them.

Hubby's driven me, as my car still isn't taxed, and my friend and I enjoy wine, so I won't drive.

I sit patiently waiting in the bar, as my phone beeps indicating Hubby has disarmed the house alarm. He's home safely. I smile.

Eventually, a little concerned by my friend's tardiness, I ring her and she tells me we're meeting tomorrow! Two intelligent women couldn't even coordinate correctly. So I need a lift home and Mr M isn't answering his mobile. No worries. I'll ring the landline.

What is our landline number? Shit! I have to ring our neighbour and ask her to knock on our door to ask SB to pick up both his phone, and me.

I could chew my arm off, but then I'd never be able to reach my bags. I decide to make a stuffed pepper as it will be ready in less than fifteen minutes.

The ricer's been used and isn't washed, so I dig out the old one. The two ricers are clearly not the same. The rice burns and I have to start over. So much for a meal in fifteen minutes. My arm is seriously under threat.

I put our landline number in my mobile's contact list.

18 May 2021

Yesterday's fears about dining out have disappeared. Perhaps my trial run has calmed my nerves. A few glasses of wine also help, although I become frustrated when I see people without masks on.

They must have a medical condition that exempts them, so why am I annoyed?

21 May 2021

I disappoint myself. No sooner have I told Hubby how much I love him, and how thankful I am, than I totally lose the plot and end up screaming, almost throwing my phone at him and stomping upstairs.

Why do I do that? I'm loathed to blame everything on the menopause, and I'm resisting HRT. I am a prick. My hubby is the best thing that ever happened to me.

I'm grateful he doesn't let me stew, instead coming to get me so we can watch the Heineken Champions Cup final between our own Leicester Tigers and Montpellier.

Tigers lost by one point and we sit in the kitchen listening to music. As the wine flows, so do our creative juices, although we aren't that creative. Our drawings look like human appendages.

Once my inner-Banksy has been exhausted, for some unknown reason that only the goddess of wine could possibly know, I invent a game based on bodily functions. Thankfully another god, Hypnos, speaks to me. I go up to bed as Hubby tells me he isn't tired and is staying in the kitchen. It's not long before I hear his footsteps. He may have been halfway up the stairs, when I shout out that if he isn't bringing me a drink, he can turn around and get one. He doesn't break stride and enters the bedroom with a balloon of Bay Leaves for me and a glass of port for himself. I love that man!

I drink mine while reading a book Sandi Toksvig has written. Hubby falls asleep without touching a drop.

I'm fortunate that I'm reading a kindle version, as I can easily look up words with which I'm not familiar. I'd rather be uneducated than get off my spreading arse to get the Oxford English Dictionary. I now know that tawdry means of poor quality. A bit like my command of the English language, it seems.

22 May 2021

SB and I have reached a compromise. I detest supermarket shopping and we need food, as I foolishly suggested we didn't need an online delivery this week.

Hubby wants me to go with him. I don't think it's appropriate to shop in couples, even though the rules have relaxed. I agree to go if I can stay in the car and read.

When did the standard of driving become so poor? Someone in front of us is indicating to turn right. Such notification would normally be welcome. Except there's a sign in front of him that tells him he has to turn left. Fortunately, he realises before proceeding the wrong way down the one-way street, and he turns left. He appropriately stops at the red light, but only temporarily. I don't know why he decided he wouldn't wait until the lights turned green before continuing his journey. It's miraculous there isn't an accident.

While Hubby is in the store, I read the headlines. There's been over fifty million potentially life-saving pricks I became distracted by a woman who parked so closely to us that she could only just open her door. She hesitated from getting out as Mr M returned. I was sure the woman would wait for us to leave, so she could more easily exit her own car. Impatiently, she squeezed herself out before we had reversed. Mr M adds one to the prick tally.

Mr M told me the checkout assistant in the supermarket spoke to him rudely. He went to customer services to complain, but isn't convinced anything will be done. I told him that he did the right thing as every little helps.

Our Eurovision entry came last, for the second consecutive year. Many believe the votes are politically persuaded. It seems that since Brexit, we've been less popular than ever.

I also read that Mr Hancock may have awarded profitable PPE contracts to his buddies. I was content to support his law-breaking when he didn't publish the contract details within the prescribed timeframes. But if he's acted without integrity, I may change my mind.

23 May 2021

It would have been the birthday of my best friend's dad today. He died on 22 August 2020. I've sent her and her mum a card to say I'm thinking of them both, at what will be a very emotional weekend.

I'm also thinking ahead to Thursday when I shall hopefully welcome my folks and hug them both, for the first time since January 2020.

I've bought balloons, bunting and table sprinkles to mark their golden wedding anniversary. I spoke with both of them today and our excitement was palpable.

Sadly, we're not also celebrating a Leicester City victory over Spurs, which would have guaranteed Champions League football next season. Nevertheless, I decided I'd like one of the club's face masks in the away colour, burgundy. I was in an on-line shop queue of one thousand, four hundred and forty people. I left.

My engine search some hours later revealed a weblink to a used mask being sold online. Who is going to buy a second-hand face mask during a pandemic, washed or not?

24 May 2021

I wasn't the only person to miss the news ten days ago, that residents in eight Indian variant hotspots, including where my parents live, shouldn't travel.

25 May 2021

There's more guidance against travelling into and out of the hotspot areas.

I knew something was awry as Mr M sat on the side of the bed looking at me with doleful eyes, as he announced this to me.

The hot tea he simultaneously brought me didn't melt the lump in my throat. I haven't hugged Mum or Dad since his seventy-eighth birthday in January 2020.

The guidance against travel isn't legally binding, although Mr M reminded me how cautious and compliant we have remained throughout. I told him that the country and we were in a different position than on 16 March 2020, when we chose to comply with the PM's lockdown request, a week before he enforced it.

Both my parents have had both vaccines. We've each had our first and we can test ourselves. Hubby was clearly not impressed while also telling me it's not his decision if Mum and Dad come or not. I cried.

My sister messaged me to say she'd help our folks take a test. I still worry that this won't pacify Mr M. It will hang over us all like a black cloud on an otherwise sunny day if they come contrary to any guidance not to.

20:46

I ring my parents overjoyed at the very recent news from the government that there aren't any localised travel restrictions. Mum's been ignoring the news anyway, adamant they are coming to see us, guidance against, or not.

I get this attitude now, one I didn't comprehend fifteen months ago. I understand that after all this time not being together as a family, and after two vaccines, Mum would stick her proverbial two fingers up to any guidance asking her not to visit her youngest daughter and son-in-law.

Our village may suffer its own restrictions soon enough.

The planning committee has approved a request to build ninety-nine houses on a nearby field. It will potentially double the traffic on the oldest and narrowest road in the village. The road has blind bends where cars frequently meet head to head requiring one to reverse. The bin lorries mount the pavements to get through, and have damaged the roadside properties while doing so. In supposed mitigation, the developer has offered to pay for some double yellow lines, which will prevent current residents parking outside their own properties, none of whom have any off-road parking. Where will they go?

The planning officer's report presented to the committee included mistakes, referencing streets that aren't even in the village. How can such a report be relied upon, especially when the consequences will be so long-lasting?

26 May 2021

04:30

I've been awake for seventy-five minutes and feel jet-lagged. Just the chance would be a fine thing.

My folks are coming tomorrow!

27 May 2021

They're coming. My parents arrive today. I have to work this morning as I'm delivering some training to our team and it was too difficult to rearrange with seven diaries to coordinate. Even if I am mid-sentence when my folks arrive, I shall be running out of the study to hug them.

We finished our training on time and Mum and Dad arrived around two minutes after.

The sun is shining, although it's possible I just haven't noticed it during otherwise darker days.

It's as if it's easier to breathe. I'm simultaneously choked by tears that involuntarily well, spilling happiness on Mum's shoulders as we hug so tightly, I can barely breathe.

Then it's time to be hugged by Dad, this man who's been over six feet tall to me, physically and metaphorically my whole life, even though he's an inch shy of six feet.

He's seventy-nine and drove one hundred and twenty-nine miles without stopping, arriving in under two and a half hours. My hero.

Mum can't find their pills. She's emptied the vanity case, ironically in vain. I do the same and then spot a small wicker basket on the floor, in which I find a buffet of medicine. We're all relieved and end up talking about Mum's Uncle who isn't well.

"I was always his favourite niece, you know. Of course, it may be because I am his only niece."

Mum, you are a legend!

28 - 30 May 2021

The days blurred as we enjoyed meals out continuing the golden wedding anniversary celebrations, as well as home-cooked food, and basking in the sun outside.

On Sunday evening, I can see from the kitchen through the glass-panelled doors into the living room, where three of the people I love most, sit watching Elvis concerts. Mr M had searched and found the shows a while back, knowing Dad in particular loves The King. I wonder if this is how parents feel when looking after their children. I doubt I could be happier. Although I doubt I'd feel the same if I had to do it every day for around eighteen years.

Dad's managed to snap a cocktail stick he was using as a toothpick. He may have dislodged what had been stuck but now has a sharp-ended mini javelin protruding from either side of a gap between his teeth. After numerous attempts with Dad in various positions, I finally manage to remove it with some tweezers. I have a new-found respect for all dentists.

31 May 2021

While SB is at golf, I spend the morning feeding the three

of us, making coffee and preparing the chicken, mushroom, and leek pie for dinner, so that I can enjoy the afternoon in the garden.

Mr M returns from golf and can't find his wallet! Thankfully I drained him of cash for yesterday's Sunday lunch tip, so he may only have lost replaceable plastic and the wallet itself.

At least he's not lost his hearing. Mum's impairment is frustrating on occasion and equally hilarious on others. Dad and I are talking about an actress whom Dad says is "up 'er own arse." Mum misheard and asked if she has "a prawn up her backside."

Many think the lady's an absolutely fabulous actress and I'm certain she doesn't have a crustacean in her rear orifice.

Dad and I sit outside in the sun. I go in to check on Mum who's fallen asleep on the sofa. Dad asks me if she's in a comfortable position. Even after fifty years of marriage and daily annoyances at her forgetfulness and apparent partial deafness, Dad only ever wants Mum to be safe and well. Perhaps that is the secret to being married for fifty years; each of you needs to be the other's priority.

In the evening, Hubby finds a film we may all enjoy and switches on the surround sound. Mum says it's like being in the cinema and all we need is popcorn. I apologise as we don't have any, and Mum tells me she doesn't eat it as it gets stuck in her teeth. We haven't any intention of repeating last night's incident, although the comedy of what Mum said is lost on her.

JUNE 2021

1 June 2021

Just as we're packing belongings into Dad's car, our fabulous DPD driver, Chris, pulls up with a delivery for next door.

I ask how his mum's recent funeral went and hope that my farewell to Mum and Dad will not be my last.

Chris told me a couple of weeks ago that he still feels his mum clipping him round the ear. I tried not to look disbelieving then, and am pleased for him that the funeral went well.

And my folks are gone. Almost simultaneously as their car turns out of sight, tears stream down my cheeks. My breath quickens and my legs start to wobble, as if I'm incapable of supporting myself without them. I am forty-seven years old, and never needed to see them more than I did this week.

There is leftover wine. Phew!

They're back! After driving for only about one mile, Dad thankfully realised he'd left his jacket behind, including his wallet. It gives us another opportunity to kiss and hug, although I hadn't wanted them to see me crying. Thank goodness I wasn't already slurping the Chablis. It's 10:10. Too early. What time is it in Oz?

Dad's jacket weighs a ton.

"It's got my wallet in it."

"It's not got mine too, has it?" asks Mr M.

Hubby goes for his second jab leaving me alone with my sorrow. I can hear footsteps and try to dismiss the ludicrous thought that my folks remain in spirit.

Perhaps Chris really does feel his mum's hand on the back

of his head. No. It can't be true, can it?

It's the window cleaner outside. Prick! (Me, not the window cleaner). My heart is racing so fast it may just be the end of me, just as there's been zero deaths for the first time since the pandemic began. Cases are rising though and other countries' vaccinations are materially behind. Surely we need to share our knowledge, expertise, and any surplus vaccines?

I also remember that other tragedy continues. A police officer accused of murdering a thirty-three-year-old woman at the beginning of March, will appear in the Old Bailey on 9 July and the trial's expected to start on 25 October. How can a five-month period from now until the trial, be justice, even when both sides need time to prepare?

Hubby joins me in the garden at around 14:00 having worked since 07:30. He's up and down like a yo-yo, checking emails and noting that every time he emerges, the sun goes in. Try sitting still, I muse.

He goes in for the last time at 17:00 to make sure he's eaten by 18:00. My legs are still too wobbly to consume no more than a faint-inducing eight hundred calories. I need a top up.

Alexa thinks I wanted bowls in the shopping, when we need washing tablets, the brand of which she confused with crockery.

I feel lost, or at least as if I need to find something I have lost. And it isn't Hubby's wallet, even though he still hasn't found it.

The house feels empty. I imagine this is how Mum felt when I left home almost thirty years ago to go to uni. Mum hid her sorrow when I used to phone home. Mine is pouring down my face like Niagara Falls.

I don't know why I wonder if this is how those giving up addictions feel. A friend empathises with my sadness, telling me it's not unreasonable after experiencing the massive high their company brought. My subsequent crash feels as like it could be as large as the financial one in 2008. The high was absolutely worth it.

I skulk in the kitchen conscious of the effect on Hubby that my emotions may have. I'm also aware Mr M may be wondering if I'm trying to avoid him. Never. I just choose to hide some emotions from him. He would accept he couldn't fully understand, having never been part of a nuclear family, adopted when only three months, and unhappy for much of his childhood.

His parents adopted another child, one of the most inspiring people I've ever met. Her husband is the same. They're both thoughtful, talented, conscientious, simply beautiful people inside and out. They welcomed me without any judgment and they are as much a part of my family as my blood sibling and her family.

And it's ok that I miss my family. It is. I can stop being upset at being upset, eat my stuffed pepper, and watch the final episode of *Mare of Easttown* with Kate Winslet.

Bollocks. I can't stop crying. Bollocks, bollocks and more bollocks (sorry, Mum – I know you'll read this). Bollocks! I looked forward to seeing Mum and Dad for four hundred and ninety-four days and was entirely unprepared for the unprecedented grief I'd feel when they left. Am I subconsciously afraid of a similar period of time before I can see them again, as nerves around the growing cases also grow? Is it in part due to the morbid recognition that one day our goodbyes will be our last, and that time is only getting closer?

A work colleague once told me that no matter how long you have with someone you love, it will never be enough.

2 June 2021

We had hoped to christen the new barbecue before tonight, but the incessant and daily downpours prevented its use until today.

And now it's raining again.

We finished eating indoors and started a heated debate about money. It's so stupid as we have, and should always have, enough for comfortable lives and retirement.

I go to bed but never one to finish the day on an argument, return to the kitchen to tell Hubby I love him. I decide to help myself to a Bay Leaves as he enjoys a port. There are two drops in the bottle. I must have returned the bottle to the cabinet, in a vain pretence that I hadn't consumed it all last time. I help myself to a glass of port.

I don't tan easily and I have some red patches about which Hubby comments. He knows that when we're on holiday, I get upset when people point out my redness. I'm not usually burnt. I just go red and eventually, and after lots of factor thirty, and even more hours in the sun, I get a slight healthy looking tan. His comments exacerbate my melancholy following his earlier suggestion while I was standing in the garden, that I should breathe in. I am not fat. I am size ten. I start to cry and Hubby hugs me commenting on his own physique, which has become a little more relaxed during the last year.

The comparisons aren't healthy and in any event, he is gorgeous. I feel the opposite.

3 June 2021

Hubby's had a reminder on his phone to wash our bedsheets. He diarised it after hearing the national average is once every three weeks.

I strip the bed and stubbornly sit outside under overcast skies, keen to continue feeling the holiday mood.

My sister has sent me a Christmas gift idea for our wonderful niece. Sis knows she's ridiculously premature and I love that she is. The item's in the sale, and we're certain our niece will adore it. What's not to be thankful about my sis sending me the suggestion?

Buying gifts now also spreads the cost and time, which avoids last minute purchases which can be regrettable, at best. Buying gifts for other people makes me smile. I imagine my niece's smiling face as she will open this one.

Buying gifts also reminds me of my maternal grandmother, which also makes me smile. She was a real woman of substance; part Greek, part bonkers, wholly adorable. She loved giving presents although often forgot what she'd bought. One year I opened something from her and Gramps, and heard her say how lovely it was, then swiftly ask what it was.

At the start of every year, she'd also buy every birthday card needed for the forthcoming twelve months. Grandma would address and stamp the envelopes, and diarise a reminder to post them.

One year, Sis and I suggested Grandma may inadvertently forget the passing of one or more of her family and friends. We pointed out that if she still sent the card, it may upset a surviving spouse or family member that opened it, and she'd have wasted her money.

4 June 2021

I walked round the golf course as Hubby and his three friends played.

The eighteenth tee usually has a view of the clubhouse. Commonly known as the nineteenth hole, the clubhouse is the only one of them I'm consistently good at.

Sadly, all that can be seen is a charred skeleton of the building that used to occupy a space, now deemed dangerous and surrounded by warning signs and fences that prohibit entry.

There isn't any news on the culprit.

It's the most I have walked in weeks and I fell asleep in the car on the way home.

When we got home, Alexa filled Mum's void, by mishearing Mr M's request for songs by Thomas Rhett. Hubby wasn't as impressed with Tammy Wynette.

I ironed the sheets from the spare room Mum and Dad slept in. Yes! I ironed even though I don't do ironing. My life has taken a serious turn for the tedious.

"It's Saturday night, and I'm ironing," I hollered.

"It's Friday!" retorted Mr M.

5 June 2021

Before the game started, I'd have taken the point we scored against Bristol in Tigers' rugby union game today. But even Bris fans admitted one of Bristol's tries shouldn't have been allowed, and are disappointed by some substitution shenanigans at the end, both of which will dominate the headlines.

Nevertheless, I enjoyed all afternoon in the garden at the end of what has been one of my favourite weeks off work, for numerous reasons.

I believe it's true that being with nature can help your mood. As I soaked up more vitamin D with a cold beverage, the sound of the breeze through the trees as the birds tweeted lazily was like a brain massage.

I'm not a medic, but I'm convinced there has to be merit in deprescribing medication and replacing it with orders to get outside, except perhaps for agoraphobics.

6 June 2021

We used the barbecue for the second time. It lashed it down!

7 June 2021

We went to see Mr M's sister and her husband, but not before I'd taken a (negative) test. My sister-in-law is selling crocheted gift bags for a charity they support and I've donated in return for some. We must have been so excited about seeing and hugging one another after so long, that we nearly left without the bags.

When I got home, my own sister had sent me photos of a letter she'd received from two of her former pupils. The letter gushed with thanks for how she'd incited their enthusiasm for English literature, *Macbeth* in particular. I've said before my sister is awesome. The letter she received helps me understand why she is a teacher. Anyone in the profession will tell you they do it to see children's potential develop, like a flower growing.

The names of so many of my former teachers came flooding back to me.

I remember Mrs Lucas, when I was four, and whose nose I sat under. I had a soft toy in school colours on my desk, made by our neighbour who used to babysit. I thought Mrs Lucas was at least eighty, and am thankful she was kind when I cried that Grandad had left me at the school gates.

I remember Mrs Sharples, when I was eight, who'd bring us treats in pink bags and claim they were from a pink fairy. Some of her pupils used to pretend they had seen the non-existent figment of our teacher's imagination.

When I was eleven, Mrs Aspden was my form teacher. Her daughter also attended the school and dated one of the best rugby league loose forwards to grace a pitch. His son now plays for the same team as he did.

And then I went to the big school where I always looked a mess with holey jumpers and ripped skirts, unaesthetically stitched using mismatching thread. I received the needlework award one year, although it was evidently to do with my theory mark and not any practical talent.

This is my letter of thanks to all my teachers.

Thank you, Mrs Fleming for bringing French to life as you tripped over fresh air, and painstakingly used tissues when pupils hid the duster, in the days when we could say blackboard.

Thank you Miss Bloomfield for taking me back to Helmshore Mill in the summer holidays, so I could rewrite a history project that was stolen from the locker I left unlocked. And thank you for believing that it had been stolen, when others didn't have your faith in me, despite my perfect track record of completing schoolwork. Thank you also for those weekends on Duke of Edinburgh expeditions.

Thank you Mrs Meadowcroft for not noticing when I accidentally called you Mrs Meadowmuck to your face.

Thank you Mrs Patefield and Mrs Kendall for animating physics, especially on a Friday afternoon when my brain was already halfway home.

Thank you Mrs Croston, the second of the two amazing headteachers I knew. Thank you for putting me up one night when my A-level exams clashed. The examining board dictated I had to be kept in quarantine after one of the exams, so that I couldn't ask my friends about any of the questions in the French aural, which I sat the following morning instead.

Thank you, Matron, for looking after me in sick bay when I was genuinely unwell, but couldn't go home as I didn't have a key. Thanks for taking me to A & E each time I fractured a finger in netball.

Thanks to my PE teachers, who encouraged me in team sports. I was fairly mediocre but good enough to make up numbers, and loud enough to spur on the quieter ones in a tough match.

Thanks to all my teachers.

This is also my apology to those I unnecessarily frustrated.

I'm sorry that school called a plumber to check all the drains, when an out of order sign was put on the toilet doors during one of my A level physics lessons.

If it's any consolation, Mrs Kendall, you told us you'd never before seen pupils produce a straight line graph from that experiment. You warned the four of us in your class that we wouldn't get the expected results, as the constant water pressure required during the experiment would be affected by anyone needing to use the toilets. And first years (now known as year twelve I think), had weaker bladders than I do.

Someone obviously thought they were using their initiative when they posted a sign that students would have to use alternative facilities.

I'm sorry, Mr Glover, that I used to walk out of French lessons to get a dictionary from the library, and then get distracted and have a coffee with my best mate. She's still my best mate, I still got a grade A in my A level, and I studied Law with French at uni. I hope that merits forgiveness.

I'm sorry, Mrs Cave, that my sister always looked neater than me, and I made your nostrils flare in anger. I hope you're pacified by my eight grade As, and two Bs, and acceptance onto a degree course with only twelve available places.

I'm sorry to all the others whose energy I sapped just a little bit more than I should have, and I am truly eternally grateful for your dedication and commitment.

Thanks to Mum and Dad for sending me to a school I loved. I even loved the lunches in the end.

Thank you to the dinner ladies, cleaners, porters, and everyone else that made the lungs of the school breathe, and helped its pupils succeed. Thank you.

8 June 2021

There are Mayflies everywhere. It's June!

It's been six months since the vaccine roll-out started and Hubby and I have been together ten years. It's longer than any career I've ever had.

He's made my life easier and happier. If only we all did that for others.

Hubby's been trying to plant some new bushes and has struck hardcore rubble. It may have been easier for the house builders to bury it there, but it's made the planting much more difficult, especially on the hottest day of the year.

9 June 2021

I'm having such a good week. Normally after a week's holiday, the return to work can be less than enjoyable. But I still feel joyous. No doubt it's helped knowing I finish early on Friday as Mr M and I are treating ourselves to two nights in one of our preferred hotels.

We've been to it in February a few times for his birthday, when we frequent the local hostelries and watch the televised rugby union matches in the annual Six Nations tournament.

It's also because I saw my folks, my sis and niece today. Sis doesn't (get paid to) work on Wednesdays. She tries to be disciplined on her day off, rather than being free labour, and often has lunch with Mum and Dad. Today, my niece joined them as she's finished her GCSEs, such as they were this year. Sis phoned en route to lunch, and my niece thanked us for the electric guitar we've given her.

I bought it years ago with an ambitious intention to teach myself to play it. Sadly, there's only one teacher in our family. Hubby and I have a guitar in Tit Corner already, and so we decided not to wait until we were dust in the ground to give mine to someone who will enjoy it. Selfishly, I also enjoyed seeing my niece's happy and thankful smile. But why should we wait until we can't see the joy a gift keeps giving?

We've sent our nephew some vouchers so he can also be treated. He video called almost immediately to say thanks. As always, his smiling face could raise the Titanic and every person's mood.

I also finished a report today that took about twelve hours to write, so I have a sense of achievement. Hopefully, my boss won't feel it needs wholesale changes.

Once I'd finished it, I took a deserved break and made some tartare to accompany tonight's fish fingers. It's one of the easiest accompaniments to make that I have consistently bought in jars for decades. That and pesto.

I don't know if I'd have ever bothered to look how to make my own if we hadn't been in lockdown. Hubby's trying to grow some basil in the garden too, so hopefully we won't need to buy a jar of either again.

It's been a fabulous day. I think I'll have a glass of wine.

A couple we know, one of whom is a GP (a proper one, Gwyneth), and the other a cardiac-trained nurse, only allow themselves to drink alcohol when they've had a good day. They don't want to confuse needing booze with needing a boost.

All the well-being courses also suggest we should really

savour a drink. We should look at it, smell it, sip it, and enjoy its taste. This apparently helps us to have a healthy relationship with alcohol.

Or you can just throw it down your neck, and prop up the insolvent economy more quickly.

10 June 2021

I can live with the report amendments my boss suggested and am part way through another that I have been asked to write.

A good friend who lives nearby, whom I haven't seen in long enough to have a baby, came round. We reminded each other we're doing great! It sounded patronising when I said it to her, but I know that her gratitude was honest. She'd happily slap me if not. Sometimes I think I need a slap, and then I remember it's frowned upon.

I ate the other half of Mr M's fasting meal. He always makes enough for two meals, and ordinarily eats the same on Tuesday and on Thursday each week. But this week he didn't have time to cook it on Tuesday so ate something else. Being philanthropic (and not wanting to waste the defrosted chicken), I offered to eat the same as him tonight. I mistakenly thought he'd made me a larger portion but was pleasantly satisfied by the five hundred or so calories. I've decided to eat the same as him on Tuesday and Thursday next week, and see if I lose any weight.

11 June 2021

At 12:20, I finished another report for one of the team who hasn't got time to write it, meaning I can take my half day's leave as booked.

We're going away for the weekend to Stamford in one of our favourite hotels. The forecast is glorious too. We asked the hotel if it could prepare a Saturday picnic for two, so we could venture to Rutland Water. It quoted fifty pounds per person. I realise it had salmon and prawns in it, but the beverage was mineral water, and I'd have expected fizz for that price. I was prepared to pay that for both of us, on the basis the hotel does exceptionally good food, but one hundred pounds is too much for a picnic. I'm not paying fifty pounds each.

It makes me wonder if the hotel has intentionally priced it prohibitively, so it doesn't have to prepare it.

Thankfully, our well-equipped neighbour has lent us a cool box that plugs into the car or into a room plug socket to keep the contents the desired temperature. We can take our own booze and will pick up some picnic food elsewhere, and save ourselves about ninety-two pounds!

Our hotel room isn't one we've stayed in before. We specifically requested an en suite with separate shower cubicle and bath, as Mr M has to stoop under showers over baths. It's on the third and top floor. For the first time, I started to appreciate how people with breathing difficulties may struggle to wear a mask. I felt out of breath after mounting the stairs carrying our luggage and regretted declining the porter's offer of assistance. I'm not as unfit as some, and still felt as if there wasn't enough oxygen in the atmosphere.

The hotel and grounds are wholly non-smoking, as they have placed more dining tables in the courtyard. Mr M's frustrated that he can't enjoy a pre-dinner cigar outside the hotel, and so we go to a nearby bar with a rooftop.

It saved us a fortune as drinks were much cheaper and also meant we appreciated the delicious wine with dinner more than we may have.

It's an absolute joy to dine knowing we don't have to clear up afterwards. Mr M orders the seafood platter for the first time and I treat myself to one of the finest medium-rare steaks I've ever tasted.

12 June 2021

I feel so refreshed after a fabulous night's sleep, awake in the knowledge that I don't have to do any washing-up today either.

We find a small shop serving Mediterranean lunch boxes and spend nineteen pounds on our picnic food. It's not a saving of ninety-two compared to the hotel's quote, but it's enough to pay for some fizz.

I've forgotten a bottle stopper, but have a brain wave. Once we've poured the first glass each, we can pour what's left of the champagne into one of our insulated water bottles that we use for cold water. Genius.

It takes less than twenty minutes to arrive at Rutland Water, one of the largest official lakes in Europe.

There are some picnic professionals spread across the vast expanse of grass. There's fixed stands on which you can put coals and cook your food, whereas some visitors have their own portable barbecues. Others have tents, marquees, paddling pools, shisha bongs and an array of children's games. A bride and groom are playing cricket and we jealously walk past a couple who remembered their foldable chairs! We spread out our rug so we have a view of the lake and watch the multitude of sailing boats.

A couple arrives not long after us. Of all the places they could choose, they sit directly behind four foot reeds, various bushes, and trees, all of which block the view of the lake. After a few hours, the gentleman stands up, walks to his left, looks briefly at the rippling water before they both leave. Odd. Very odd.

It's almost as odd as the man in a black puffer jacket with hood up, when it must be at least twenty-five degrees. He seems to be trying to make eye contact with a seated woman wrapped so tightly in a blanket, it looks like she wouldn't be able to stand up.

After listening on the radio to the Tigers beat Wasps, we head back to the hotel. We've parked for one minute more than five hours, which costs an extra, disproportionate two pounds. At least we saved on the picnic. It's been one of the loveliest days in a long time, seeing groups of friends and family gather safely outdoors, enjoying games, reading, or people watching.

Most people respected the rules not to play music, or at least kept the volume at a reasonable level, as we did with the rugby commentary. More importantly, everyone seemed to be respecting each other's space.

The only noise most people will have heard will have been the rustling of kites, the odd speed boat engine and an occasional child's whimper if a sibling wasn't playing nicely.

Another stunning meal marks the end of a fabulous day enjoying the best that England has to offer.

13 June 2021

We were back home well before the first of England's Euro 2020 matches, and felt as if we'd had a real holiday. I suggested to Hubby what could be a great quiz question in a century or so.

"What year was the Euro 2020 football tournament played?"

I camped in the garden with a portable speaker so I could listen to the commentary on the radio. I refused to be indoors watching TV when it was twenty-five degrees in the shade.

For the first time ever, England started the tournament with a win, and Croatia with a defeat. It sounded like quite a promising performance by The 'Land!

14 June 2021

I'm not surprised that the relaxation of restrictions has been postponed, and won't now be effective in a week.

I shouldn't be surprised that people still made bookings for events from 21 June onwards that they now can't postpone, cancel, or obtain refunds for. We were all told that 21 June was the earliest we'd have more freedom, yet many proceeded to book non-refundable events. According to the polls though, the majority of people think the Prime Minister has made the right decision. I suppose that could be a majority of fifty-two percent to forty-eight.

I've postponed the date three of our family's households will meet for lunch, by three weeks to 25 July 2021. Thankfully, we may be granted freedom earlier than in other countries. Only China, USA, Brazil, and India have issued more vaccines by number. We're ahead of all of them based on the number per hundred of the population. That will, in part, be because we started vaccinating people much sooner than most other countries. It looks as though only Russia beat us on that, and only by three days. Even so, we've done one hundred and six vaccines per hundred people, and Russia has only done twenty-three.

15 June 2021

I am trying Hubby's fasting regime properly for the first time this week. I did feel hungry around noon and just before our evening meal but then felt quite bloated.

16 June 2021

Why do I feel really heavy this morning?

17 June 2021

So far this week, every day I have done thirty minutes of weeding in my lunch break. The garden's never looked better in the eight years we've lived here. When I'm working away from home again, I'll miss the time I can spend tending it and sitting in it.

As I put away the dinner plates, I realised that Mr M uses the same dish at least twice a week, and it was in the least accessible place in the cupboard, on the bottom shelf at ankle height. Conversely, the cake tins I use once a year at Christmas were on a higher, more accessible shelf. We've had this kitchen for two years and never thought to rearrange the cupboards until now. I wonder what holds my ears apart at times.

18 June 2021

SB has the most horrendous swelling on his elbow. Maybe it's from constantly trying to reach in and out of almost inaccessible cupboard spaces.

19 June 2021

Our wonderful neighbour helped me trim the bush that had started to spread into their garden. SB wouldn't trust me with the hedge trimmers and despite his painful elbow, neatened the rest. He doesn't like overgrown bushes.

20 June 2021

Fathers' Day

I spoke to my dad and annoyingly his gift hasn't arrived!
As we can't go for lunch with them and my sister on 4 July to celebrate, I've invited my folks to stay with us that weekend anyway.

21 June 2021

It's the longest day of the year. We've put the heating on!

22 June 2021

The England football team marches on with a one-nil victory to top the group. Italy is the only other nation not to have conceded a goal.

24 June 2021

News breaks of Britney Spears's twenty-minute monologue to the judge in her ongoing court case. She's asking the court to remove her father as her conservator. In America, the courts will grant conservatorship for individuals who cannot make their own decisions. Since 2008, Britney has been deemed to be one such person.

Everything she's done over the last thirteen years has required approval. She can't have more children, get married, or make decisions about her own finances which are paying her father's legal bills. She doesn't seem to have any rights. I wonder what she thinks of anti-maskers who claim that their rights are being violated.

I wonder too what Valérie Bacot would think. The forty-year old French mother of four, will soon be in court, accused of murdering her husband and father of their four children. According to her book, the former lover of Valérie's mother started abusing Valérie when she was only twelve. He was jailed for abusing her, but returned to the family home after his release, and recommenced the abuse.

At seventeen, when Valérie became pregnant by him, her mother made them both leave the house. Valérie had nowhere else to go, so she married him, and the abuse worsened. Her husband forced her to prostitute herself, sometimes fifteen times a night, while he watched through a peep hole.

Valérie and her four children all lived in fear of him. They were followed if they went anywhere and were constantly humiliated. She shot him dead when she feared he may start abusing his own daughter. With the help of at least one of her children, she buried his body in a forest, and was eventually arrested for his murder.

She may go to jail. In England, there is a legal doctrine of diminished responsibility. It absolves an accused person of at least part of the liability for a criminal act on the basis that the person suffered a substantial impairment to responsibility. If Valérie's story is true, the poor woman and her children have suffered enough already. But I'm not sure her decision to bury his body without confessing will help her case. Whether she's freed or not, she may never truly be free. Would she object to being asked to wear a mask, or to avoid travel to certain countries temporarily, in return for her liberty from jail?

25 June 2021

I told Mr M when I woke that it seemed longer than three weeks since I washed the sheets.

"It is. The reminder popped up on my phone on Wednesday!"

Valérie Bacot has been found guilty of murder and sentenced to four years in jail, three of which are suspended. She's already served one year while awaiting trial, so she is free to walk out of the courtroom. I hope that her life really will begin at forty.

26 June 2021

I went to see my two best friends today. One I met at school in Blackburn and the other I met when I first started my career over twenty years ago in Leicester. Coincidentally, they live about ten minutes from each other.

I forgot to give one of them some shower caps I took with me, and left my water bottle in the living room of the other. I also found that I instantly forget what I am saying if I am interrupted, but I remembered that seeing mates is fabulous.

27 June 2021

Dad rang to tell me his gift has finally arrived. He thinks I'm psychic as the gilet I've sent him is just what he's been looking for. I love it when that happens.

28 June 2021

It's the first day of the Wimbledon tennis tournament in two years. It's raining.

29 June 2021

England beat Germany for the first time in fifty-five years in a knockout tie, two-nil. That scoreline's got a familiar ring to it.

30 June 2021

08:45

I'm not sure whether it's because of last night's victory that I am so happy or because my folks are coming tomorrow.

Why should I care? I'm happy, I know it and I may just clap my hands.

It could be because I'll speak to my sister later to wish her happy birthday. I'll also find out what we bought this time last year and wrapped for her birthday. We weren't able to give gifts to her in person and they were too heavy to post. We arranged for other gifts to be delivered directly to her last year, and kept the original purchases until we could hand deliver them as planned. I've forgotten what we bought and hope there's nothing perishable.

14:40

I am in agony. I went for a coil removal and replacement but the doctor couldn't find the existing one.

Those recent stories of women screaming in pain may not be because of anything exceptional in their cases. It is a painful procedure, but at least our NHS offers the service, for which I'd happily pay the one hundred pounds each coil costs.

I felt for the doctor today. She devotes her life to making sure I can enjoy mine, and was genuinely concerned about any pain I may be in. I thought she had the hardest part.

By the time I got home, I felt too sick to have any wine on wine Wednesday, which was a bummer. I like wine.

July 2021

1 July 2021

My folks have safely arrived after a delay following a crash on the motorway in which someone died.

It doesn't take long before Mum has us all in stitches while watching the tennis.

"Ooh, that's er....! Is it him?"

"Nothing like him!" I tell her. I have absolutely no idea about whom she's thinking, not least as he doesn't look like anyone, except himself!

Hubby showed Dad a video of Leicester City Football Club's new training facility that cost eighty-three million pounds.

"Eighty-three million," squawked Mum. "For a field?"

To be fair, she was on her second gin at that point, and the prospect of any logical thinking had gone with the first one.

2 July 2021

As seems to be usual with Mum and me nowadays, we ended up comparing menopause notes.

"My hot flushes didn't last long," says the seventy-three year old.

"What are you on about, you lunatic?" asks Dad. "You're still having them!"

Mum can't find her phone and I ask her if she uses the shoulder phone bag we bought her for Mothers' Day this year.

"I don't want to lose it," she replies, almost apologising for not using our gift.

Maybe you should put your marbles in it Mum.

3 July 2021

Four-nil to the Eng-er-land! Four-nil to the Eng-er-land!

4 July 2021

Mr M treats us all to lunch at one of our favourite restaurants. It's wonderful to see the safely distanced tables fully occupied. I hope I always remember what a privilege it is to dine out.

5 July 2021

My folks have gone.

6 July 2021

Our Prime Minister has announced there may not be any legal restrictions at all when they are lifted. He will leave it up to our common sense whether we choose to wear masks, socialise in numbers, or maintain social distance.

After over fifteen months of restrictions, I thought I'd be excited. I'm the opposite and can't remember when I felt this nervous.

I may need to travel to clients' from September onwards. I wasn't overly concerned when I mistakenly thought the relaxation of restrictions applied to the number of people meeting. I thought we'd still be obliged to cover our faces and keep our distance. I will continue to do so, but the prospect of being on a busy train or tube with people who'll happily and openly cough and splutter isn't appealing. One of our team has Covid and she's had both jabs.

7 July 2021

It's sixteen years since four coordinated suicide attacks targeted London commuters during the rush hour. I was in the Galapagos Islands, incommunicado from anyone at home. We had stopped to collect more passengers from one of the islands and so were allowed to disembark. Most of the passengers headed straight for an internet café. My boyfriend and I chose to get a coffee first. As we sat people watching, we saw an Australian couple from the boat bounding towards us.

"Have you heard the news? Do you want the good news or the bad news first?"

Without allowing us to answer, they seamlessly blurted that the United Kingdom had won its quest to host the 2012 Olympics, and that London had been bombed. My boyfriend lived in the outskirts and worked fairly centrally, so we immediately dashed to contact friends and family. Thankfully, everyone we knew was safe but I remember the sombre feeling, nevertheless. Fifty-six people died.

18:00

I went to the local chippy as neither of us fancied cooking before England's semi-final tonight. Oh my goodness. I hate queueing! I would happily live a life where everything is delivered to my door on demand. If only that was possible with fish and chips.

We won! We beat Denmark by two goals to one, after a fantastic performance against a strong team.

It's the first time in fifty-five years that the men's England football team has been in a major final. We're still singing a song about thirty years of hurt. No wonder children struggle with arithmetic.

8 July 2021

Mr M's playing golf today instead of Friday. I must remember that tomorrow is not Saturday. I've got my mid-year appraisal in the morning, so it wouldn't be a good time to accidentally not turn up.

10 July 2021

We host a couple of friends from 13:00 and are thankful the weather is far better than forecast. We would have been allowed to go indoors if it had rained but it somehow feels more relaxed being outdoors.

They left about the same time as our neighbour appeared in his garden with a glass of red and a cigar. We can see him as neither of us have replaced the fence panel we removed so we could enjoy drinks and chats at distance in our respective gardens. We nip through the gap and end up stopping for around three hours.

It was much more difficult to make the return journey home without falling in the bushes.

11 July 2021

We met my sister-in-law and her husband for brunch. It's our belated silver wedding anniversary gift to them and always such a pleasure to see them.

It's also a pleasure to hear that a woman will umpire the men's Wimbledon tennis final for the first time. I'm flabbergasted. Rugby has had female officials for a number of years, as has snooker. It seems strange that tennis is so far behind, especially when the All England Tennis Club's patron is the Duchess of Cambridge.

It's also the first time an Italian has been in the final. He couldn't outplay Djokovic who won in four sets. It's his twentieth singles Grand Slam, equalling the record shared with Federer and Nadal.

Sadly for us and the rest of England, Italy is victorious in one of today's finals. England lost the Euros 2020 final on penalties after missing three.

I'm sobbing like a schoolgirl whose pigtails have been maliciously cut off. Meanwhile Sir Richard Branson couldn't be happier having reached the edge of space on the rocket plane that his company has been developing for seventeen years. We've been waiting fifty-five for a major tournament win!

It seems we may wait at least as long again until racism is eradicated. Is it not shameful that the three players who missed penalties are being subject to racist comments? Shouldn't they be congratulated for reaching the final? Perhaps the perpetrators will be banned from all live sport for the rest of their lives.

12 July 2021

The grief of losing still casts a sombre mood over us. Hubby suggested we watch a film to try to distract us.

"If it's crap, we can turn it off!"

"Thanks Hubby. At least it won't end on penalties."

The distraction only lasts as long as a scene in which the name of the street on which the two main characters live is shown. Southgate Crescent. Aaargh.

13 July 2021

My boss is on holiday. She told me she won't be responding to messages as she's going out.

Colin Pitchfork will also be out soon. The Leicestershire baker raped and murdered two schoolgirls around forty years ago when he was twenty-three, and was the first person to be convicted using DNA evidence.

His capture followed an unprecedented screening of five thousand men. Despite Pitchfork persuading a colleague to take the test for him, he was caught. Someone overheard a man in the pub saying he'd taken the test for someone else, and Pitchfork was jailed in 1988. He left his wife and two children behind, and left the victims' families without their children. The Parole Board said last month it was safe to release the sixty-one-year-old. The government sought to challenge the Parole Board's decision, in vain.

While in prison, he's apparently furthered his education to degree level and is an expert at transcribing music into braille.

Barbara Ashworth, mother of Dawn, one of the victims, said he can't hurt her anymore. Will people angered that a life sentence allows parole, or will potential vigilantes, turn a blind eye when he is released?

Will the taxpayer fund a change of identity or appearance, and ongoing protection so that the public is blinded to his true identity? Is that another price of justice? Is it justice? Should he have forfeited any second chance when he killed a second time?

14 July 2021

Three days left until a week off, and the weather forecast is for increasing temperatures. The last minute requests to do things before I finish on Friday are also climbing, and I may not be able to respond to them all. What's the worst that can happen?

15 July 2021

My usually reliable printer and laptop decide they need some attention from our IT department on the penultimate day before my holiday.

While I try to keep myself from drowning in IT woes that have taken ninety minutes of my day to resolve, floods in Europe cause destruction and death. We can only hope it somehow drowns the 'vid just as the Great Fire of London burnt The Plague in 1666.

16 July 2021

I can't recall looking forward to a week on holiday as much as I am. I thought I'd be desperate to board a plane, to tip waiters in Euros as I sipped another cocktail on a poolside lounger in a foreign land.

Instead, I have other plans. I intend to spend the mornings doing whatever jobs in the garden or house may be required, before sitting in the sunshine reading.

I feel tipsy after my first glass of fizz which isn't like me and it doesn't stop me having some more with our neighbours, either side of the delicious chilli I somehow rustled up.

17 July 2021

A couple of friends came over for a BBQ. I didn't drink.

18 July 2021

Why am I incapable of enjoying time off work without looking for work? I'm sitting in the garden staring at trees that need a trim, and bushes that need pruning.

Perhaps it's subconscious guilt that while I sit basking, hundreds are dying in horrific floods in Germany and Belgium. Perhaps if I do something, the guilt will wash away.

In great news, all UK adults have been offered a first jab and over forty-six million have had it. That's almost eight-eight percent of the adult population and it's been achieved one day ahead of the government's target. Almost sixty-eight percent have had both.

It's been only eight months since the first vaccination. There are swathes of eligible adults that haven't had either jab because they can't afford the bus fare to get to a vaccination centre.

Our PM also can't go out, as he has to self-isolate from today, and ironically, our recently appointed Health Secretary has tested positive too.

19 July 2021

Quite rudely on the first weekday of my holiday, the neighbour's rooster woke me at 05:30. Another neighbour's been sitting in our kitchen telling us she feels unwell and we should both isolate. Thankfully, that was a dream. Sadly, the rooster wasn't.

Hubby's gone to golf and I declined the offer to walk round

the course as I sometimes do when on holiday. Instead, I spent a couple of hours trimming the bushes and trees that are growing over the fence that separates our garden from those perpendicular to it at the backs of the neighbouring row of houses.

Each of those houses has really long gardens and sadly, the ends near our fence are treated like the local tip (without the need for prior booking). Trolleys, old treadmills, and overgrown foliage occupy what could be space for children to play, or for dogs to catch balls.

It frustrates me that the neighbours' untidiness impacts on us. Our fence bulges in parts with the force of what grows on the other side. I regularly trim what starts to grow over our shed, to make sure branches don't navigate themselves under the felt on its roof, causing damage and leaks, necessitating a costly replacement.

After two hours of trimming, with rivers running down my back that brings my thoughts back to those flooded in Europe, I sit down to distract myself with a book. I've downloaded another memoir recommended in The Times. I don't know why. It's the tragic story of a sixteen-year-old, severely injured in a hit and run as he walked with two friends. He was nearest the road and took the full force of the vehicle that drove off, leaving him lying on the road bleeding.

I think of Dad who's always walked roadside. I understand Victorian men did so to protect the ladies' full skirts from mud splashes kicked up by the horses and carts. My dad walks roadside so that if a car veers, he'd take the brunt, protecting anyone else with whom he walked. That's heroic. My dad's a hero, although he'd deny it. I think he thinks you have to die to be a hero.

The book I'm reading told by the victim's sister, doesn't have a miraculous ending. The only happiness is that following her brother's death, eight years after the accident and after a court case, her and her family have started to have some moments of living without grief or guilt.

The careless driver came forward and paid one hundred and eighty pounds in court costs!

20 July 2021

I'm determined not to spend all day every day doing chores. I committed each morning to various jobs, including putting the second spare room back together after having the feature wall papered.

Hubby's done a tip run. It's his first day on holiday when he would normally be working, and he's bored. He's indoors watching a show he's seen very recently. I struggle with his boredom, given what needs doing indoors. I'm determined to leave him alone and get on with my holiday in equal measure. I think I'll avoid more memoirs and read some racy sleaze.

21 July 2021

We woke up to news that golf ball-sized hail has written off cars and broken windows, causing house floods around twenty miles from us. I appreciate being spared.

We enjoyed a lovely evening outside with friends who live not far. He renovated our kitchen and dining room two years ago and we've hardly used the living room since.

Once they left, I wondered if they'd have been so complimentary about our culinary expertise, if we'd served homemade burgers and marinaded chicken skewers indoors one cold Saturday evening. What is it about eating al fresco that makes basic food seem special? And why do we call it al fresco when the Italian translation means in prison?

22 July 2021

Even though it's Thursday, Hubby decides against fasting today, potentially regretting the rebellious insistence to stay up until 02:00, just because we're on holiday!

23 July 2021

We got home after Hubby's round of golf and he told me

one of the jokes he found on a social media page.

"Fifty-two years ago tomorrow, the Apollo 11 mission landed on the moon. May their names live on forever. Neil Armstrong! Buzz Aldrin! And the other bloke!"

I declared my embarrassment at failing to recall his name and carried on eating.

Three minutes later, Hubby spouted "Michael Collins!"

"Who's Michael Collins?"

The penny dropped as I announced that we'd missed the opening ceremony to The Olympics.

Hubby's most recently acquired watch allows two different time zones.

"I'll set one to Hong Kong for The Olympics," he proudly declared.

"They're in Japan, babe!"

24 July 2021

It's supposed to rain today and we'd already previously decided we'd venture into the town centre. A bit of precipitation doesn't deter me, not least as I've been waiting to be able to take a silk scarf to the dry cleaner for a long time. I also need to collect a watch that's had a new battery.

We know the dry cleaner, who tells us business is (not surprisingly) very slow. Perhaps more worryingly for his future, he tells us that a solicitor had been in earlier in the week, wearing jeans. They don't need dry cleaning. That said, I bought a pair with seventy percent off recently, and the care label dictates dry cleaning only. I have contemplated risking them in the machine, but if they shrink anymore I won't get my post 'vid thighs and arse in them.

25 July 2021

For the first time in eighteen months, my sister and her family, our parents and we were able to have lunch together. Hubby and I found somewhere almost equidistant between my sister and us. We'd gone to it in error one time we were supposed to meet family at a place of the same name.

We all agreed to try it given its perfect location and it was much more spacious than the venue at which we'd previously dined. It was a perfect day. We couldn't fault the food, venue, or service, and being with all my family was an occasion I sometimes feared may never happen again. So many won't get that chance again.

My nephew seems to have advanced eighteen years, not months. He's going to be a lawyer because, "It's very prestigious and you never know what you're gonna get!" Coincidentally the bookshelves behind our table had various editions of the All England Law Reports. I was reminded that he's not even ten, when he declared that he'd found a spelling mistake. I didn't have the heart to tell him otherwise.

My niece had come dressed all in black in case she had to go from lunch straight to one of her two waitressing jobs. My parents didn't let me wear black until I was sixteen, as they felt it was too old for a child. Then I remembered, my niece is sixteen. How did that happen?

26 – 30 July 2021

I've navigated my first week at work after my holiday.
Emails responded to – 3,451 (ish).
Telephone calls answered – only four (a sign of the times).
Emails left in inbox still to be dealt with – three.
Time it will take to deal with said emails – approximately fifty-six hours!
Summer seems to be bypassing us. But I know I have been enjoying myself, rather than being buried in my phone, scrolling through screens of negativity and cat pictures. I've tasted the food, appreciated the wine, and lived.

30 July 2021

21:00

Bridget Christie is on QI.

"Is she related to what's-her-face that's married to that footballer?"

"You mean Christine Bleakley" replies Hubby, never ceasing to amaze me with his understanding of the inner-workings of my brain.

31 July 2021

Mr M's been trying to hang the new light fitting in the second spare room, ahead of both spare rooms being used by VIPs tonight. He fitted the one in the first spare room a few weeks ago. Today, he had to remind himself how, by unscrewing it from the ceiling. He changed the other and both worked fine as they dangled, and then ceased working once screwed flush to the ceiling.

He's gutted and isn't pacified that our guests will be too legless by the time they hit the sack to even care that they need to use bedside lamps instead. On the other hand, I was as excited by the prospect of having friends stay the night, as a child about to have their first sleep-over.

We all responsibly took negative tests first. Our friends arrived adorned with flowers, drinks, smiles and warm hearts that would melt the polar ice caps. Conversations quickly splintered then regrouped in a way that's impossible on video calls.

The wine flowed as the games continued. I broke out the dinner party ice breaker questions my sister bought me some years ago. I was asked to describe my worst date. I was crying from laughing so hard as I tried to tell the story. At the time, I had just cried.

Prior to the date, I'd spoken every night with someone I'd met online. I bought a new laptop with camera so we could see each other. After around six months, we agreed to meet. He was from Scotland and I was keen to see more of the country. We agreed to meet near Inverness, which wasn't his home town, so had some neutrality. He was handsome, witty, and worked on oil rigs.

On arrival, I wasn't amused that he refused to drive into the airport to collect me, as he'd have to pay. So I had to walk, carrying my bags, to where he was parked. On first sight of each other, I could have laughed at the irony of him accusing me of lying about my height. I wondered what I had let myself in for, as I told him I was genuinely five foot six, and curious to find myself almost eye-balling a man who'd told me he was six foot three.

I honestly thought he was joking when I asked what he fancied doing for dinner that night. He told me he'd already eaten with his folks at 16:30 and would take me to a supermarket so I could buy a sandwich.

I also loaded the basket with some wine. I might have been forgiven if I had wanted to smash one over his head, when he said it was ludicrous to spend almost six pounds on one bottle. Of course, I'd never dream of intentionally wasting wine, or six pounds.

I bought two bottles. One for each night of the weekend, which proved necessary. He didn't make any offer to pay for my dinner.

The following morning, he knocked on my room door and promptly announced he had to go back to the oil rig, leaving me in a strange place for around forty hours before my miserable flight home.

For some bizarre reason, recounting the story was possibly the most hilarious part of the evening. Friends make a bad situation more palatable. I'd not realised how much we'd missed hosting and entertaining people until the tears fell down my cheeks as we roared at a story that I wouldn't have believed could be laughable.

AUGUST 2021

1 August 2021

Mr M and I enjoyed a Sunday of lie-ins and leftovers. I felt rude I hadn't woken before our guests had to leave. But we'd only been in bed for around five hours. I took it as a sign of our strong friendships, that they were comfortable to let themselves out. They did so without waking us, for which I could have hugged them again. They even took time to remake the beds. We do the same when we visit theirs. Why do we do that?

2 August 2021

A busy week beckons despite still working from home. I must remember to put some makeup on for the video calls, to mask the ghostlike effect of not being abroad for so long.

3 August 2021

Hubby is stiff after golf yesterday and I remind him that getting older is better than the alternative.

He's ecstatic that the electrician has told us he'd done nothing wrong when trying to hang the spare room lights. Apparently, it's a design flaw that most have interior fittings that don't properly hold the necessary wires. The sparky sorted it all in around ten minutes in exchange for a note. We've bought two more of the same lights for our bedroom and dressing room and promptly agreed we'd ask the electrician to fit them. Life's too short.

4 August 2021

My friend from next door and I went out for dinner to break up the week. We both looked forward to dining together without having to clear up afterwards.

Hubby hosted her partner and then both men arrived at the restaurant at 20:30 to pick us up. The four of us enjoyed another drink back at ours, and then my exhausted husband retired to bed.

I cleared up.

Hubby stirred as I crawled into bed and we both re-descended so he could have a cup of tea. He immediately thanked me for tidying up, which pacified my simmering annoyance that I had washed-up after the men. I sighed with relief that I hadn't launched down his throat for leaving it to me, especially given he'd been our taxi service.

5 August 2021

I went out for dinner again, this time to meet a friend from Leicester uni who lives in Woking. He's stopping in Leicester with his lovely partner and two children. They've been to the National Space Centre and are en route to a car museum in Derby tomorrow. He's recently been made redundant and it reminds me that being exhausted from work is better than being exhausted looking for work.

6 August 2021

Last night I dreamt Hubby had died. I was panicking that I wouldn't be able to let all his friends know as I couldn't access his phone contacts. He's just bought a new phone and it's accessed via face recognition. In my dream, I refused to let the ambulance crew take him away, as I needed his face to be able to keep unlocking his phone screen.

We both desperately hope it isn't a premonition. Hubby tells me I'd be able to unlock it with his usual six-digit PIN anyway, so there's no need to panic that he'd be dead!

7 August 2021

Gramps would be one hundred and two today, if he hadn't passed away fifteen years ago. It feels fitting that we're going to watch cricket at Trent Bridge with friends we met almost a decade ago on cricket tour in Sri Lanka. My grandad drew me a cricket field with all the fielding positions when I was little. I still have it.

The weather forecast this week has been up and down, so we're blessed to watch ninety uninterrupted overs until 19:00, not long before the heavens open. Our captain scored a very impressive century. I was less than impressed by the lack of mandatory safety measures. Very few people wore masks despite requests to do so while moving around, and I only saw one sanitiser station. There weren't any one-way systems in operation which meant it looked no different than being at Trent Bridge pre-pandemic.

When I go to Lords on Thursday, I understand all attendees will need to respect one-way systems and wear masks unless exempt. I didn't expect that I may feel safer in our capital.

8 August 2021

It rained all day at Trent Bridge, heightening my feeling of good fortune at being there yesterday.

We picked up my pre-booked train tickets for my trip to Lords on Saturday, watched two films, and enjoyed my fish pie. After a day surrounded by fifteen thousand people yesterday, spending time with each other was bliss.

9 August 2021

I did the ironing. Perhaps it shouldn't be noteworthy, but it is, and I will note it. It may never happen again.

10 August 2021

I washed my hair using shower gel, then my body using shampoo. I hope the latter's claim that it promotes hair growth, is false.

Mr M feels guilty I did the ironing. We agreed when he left full-time (paid) work, he would do the housework. I know that can be a full-time position, which in addition to his self-employment, would equate to more than my career. I feel it's only fair to contribute. I do most of the weeding and he always mows the lawns. He cleans the cars and I do the house, wondering why every man I know refuses to clean the toilets. Hubby polishes the kitchen granite fifteen times a day and I make the beds. It works.

I realised it's been over a year since I posted anything on Facebook. I intended to take a break from it for a month last August and have never returned. Admittedly, Hubby keeps me up to date on local village news, found only by trawling pages and pages of food, drink and cat pictures before finding anything of importance or relevance.

One of my best friends keeps her account as her son's school uses it to communicate with parents about sporting and other events he has to attend. I remember arranging nights out with my friends when I was at school. We'd agree at lunchtime on Friday, what time that night, and where we would meet. We turned up, on time. We told each other we looked great, without taking a selfie and filtering it and then concluding the same. I remember those days with happy memories. I cannot say the same of much of what I read on social media. A lot of my friends' sentiments about social media mirror my own, but they keep their accounts, despite no real reason for doing so. Why? What do they fear they will miss?

11 August 2021

Our friends next door invited us for dinner. He's an inventive cook and likes it to be aesthetically pleasing. He tried to design our pancake starters to suit our tastes. Hubby's was shaped into a golf club and balls and mine was a cheesy topped nob! We took photos and Hubby posted them on social media.

When we got home, I briefly contemplated not taking a lateral flow test, as a positive result would prevent me going to Lords tomorrow. Then I remembered I am not selfish and took a test. Maybe there was an element of selfishness about that, as I'd feel guilty if I may have unwittingly spread the virus.

12 August 2021

It's the first day of the second test against India. Despite being disappointed by the lack of safety measures at the last match I attended, I realised I hadn't been as concerned as I might have been, or as bothered. Was I becoming flippant about the risks because I wanted to, and finally got to watch some cricket? Did I feel safer because seventy-five percent of adults have had both vaccines? Was I just fed up with unsustainable restrictions? Or was I so thrilled our niece got top marks in all her exams, that nothing else seemed important?

I still wore a mask along with a minority. The match continued until 19:00 due to some early rain requiring extended play. We had to leave just before the end, to get to the restaurant on time.

I tried to order my steak tartare without the egg on top, but the waiter was adamant I should have it. Perhaps unexpectedly, it wasn't the Frenchman who surrendered, and he'd been right to be insistent.

I felt morose when I left my friends so I could catch the train home. Did my brain fear I may not see them for another two years?

13 August 2021

I sat down at 15:30 to enjoy the cricket on my day off. I've been changing the sheets in the spare room and ours, washing yesterday's dishes, emptying the washing machine, and refilling it, hoovering, emptying bins, and polishing the granite. I also thought about ironing (again), but opened a bottle of white like a normal person on holiday.

The orange and blue rectangular cushions I ordered for the blue room arrived. They add just the splash of colour needed to negate spending more money to replace the magnolia bedding.

When I was choosing them, I remembered one of my art lessons which taught us that opposite colours work well together. Opposite colours consist of one of the three primary colours, and the opposite colour is the combination of the remaining two primary colours. Therefore, red is opposite to green, as green is made from yellow and blue. Yellow is opposite to purple, which is made from blue and red. Blue is opposite to orange. I have always remembered that art lesson, and appreciate the ongoing relevance of it, especially when buying soft furnishings.

Is that why we say opposites attract?

14 August 2021

Mr M finished the ironing before I was up. He's decided to make coronation chicken. When I asked him what ingredients he needed, he told me he puts coronation in it.

"The flowers?" I asked.

"No, you nob! That's carnations!"

As I watched the cricket in my dressing gown, I misheard the commentator referring to a thick edge, and thought she'd said dickhead.

15 August 2021

We went for lunch at a pub nearby. We knew its pre-'vid chef had left, and thought we'd try it as we've always liked the staff and customers and décor.

Unfortunately, we were disappointed, and the owner took the constructive criticism as intended. We'll try again, but wonder how many places are suffering to get and keep experienced staff.

This country rarely recognises working in the hospitality sector as a profession of which workers can be proud, often receiving no more than minimum wage. Yet, we expect European standard service, where staff train for years and work in the same venue for decades.

Many that worked in the sector have returned to their birth countries post-Brexit, and others are leaving to start university. I wonder how many Brits that believed others had taken their jobs, have stepped into the void left by their departure.

16 August 2021

My sister and family are arriving this week. I'm simultaneously excited and nervous that I'll have overlooked something as I've fallen out of the habit of planning for such occasions.

17 August 2021

Apparently there's over one million job vacancies. It's great to read that employers are recruiting again as the economy starts a long road to hopeful recovery. How long will it be before we appeal to other countries for workers, as we did in the 1950s and 60s when we couldn't fill nursing and bus driver posts from our own labour pool?

18 August 2021

Another colleague has resigned to take early retirement, realising there's more to life than work. If there is a positive from the pandemic, it's that some have reconsidered their priorities and taken positive decisions sooner than they would have. I am pleased for her.

I'll be following suit as soon as the pension pot numbers stack up. Which reminds me to buy a lottery ticket.

Hubby left a thirty-five-year professional career five years ago. We've both felt the health benefits from his reduced stress levels, and are blessed it didn't cause financial worries. Our nation seems to be more concerned by overloaded animals than by the friends around us mentally crumbling under the pressure of their workloads.

I know people who thrive on work. They're like lemmings getting out of bed each morning, itching to stroke their laptop keys or to walk into a (virtual) meeting room. I also know and see people having their motivation slowly drawn out of them, like a syringe taking a blood donation, except the motivation doesn't replenish itself. They weakly get out of bed as if they'd given eight pints of haemoglobin.

People make fortunes selling courses about maintaining motivation and about what motivates people. How hard can it be? I think many would recognise that saying thank you goes a long way. Have we forgotten about manners? Did we use them all up before we fought over the last toilet roll or bag of pasta? Do any of us remember parents insisting children said please and thank you? Has Alexa rendered Ps and Qs redundant, by doing whatever anyone rudely demands?

19 August 2021

It would have been our friend's birthday today. She died on 16 October 2020. I remember watching the funeral on zoom. It was an experience I'd never expected to encounter and one which, nine months later, has a morbid semblance of normality. I remember staring at the screen, transfixed by the purple coffin. It's serenity was a contradiction of her exuberant life.

As her husband said then, we hadn't expected her to be carried off so quickly. I sobbed when I heard the news. I carried on sobbing until I made myself stop. Then I started sobbing again in December and couldn't stop.

I remember feeling cheated. We generally saw each other quarterly, the last time being her husband's sixtieth in December 2019. Covid struck just as we'd have been due to meet up again. The world as we knew it changed overnight and we never saw her again.

We couldn't go to the funeral. I lamely believed our physical presence could have brought light to the most bereaved in their darkest hours. That's when I realised funeral attendance is as much to help the attendee.

I remember going immediately back to work after the remote funeral. I didn't eat crustless sandwiches while reminiscing with the deceased's family and friends. I worked. I should have been sharing stories of her carrying two handbags when she couldn't decide which to wear. I worked. We should have told tales of her relentless charitable work. I worked. We should have mused while sipping fizz at how she drank so much without ever being hungover. I worked, and the effervescence of a fitting ceremony soon became flat.

My sister and family arrived at 16:15. Within seconds my sombre mood was punctured with laughter and chatter with my nine-year-old nephew, still buzzing from an afternoon in an adventure park.

He offered me a sweet.

"Were they tuppence each?"

"Aunty, that was in the old days," and he started to show me videos of Doctor Pimple Popper. I pushed the sweets away.

20 August 2021

While I'm making my breakfast smoothie, my nephew says he'd like a blender so he can make iced drinks.

"We get like a kilo of ice with the shopping but Mum goes through that with all her gin and tonics."

21 August 2021

They've gone.

And they may have taken all my energy with them. My lethargy could have something to do with staying up until 03:00 putting the world to rights with Hubby and my sister's fiancé.

I put the first load in the machine and wonder how anyone stays on the parenting treadmill. How do they get laundry, cooking, cleaning, and everything else done, while their offspring continue to create laundry and appetites?

It's a full-time job. Historically, one person, usually the woman, used to do it while the other went out to earn a living. Over time, women started to work outside the home. During the war, they'd been called upon to assist and it can only have helped society realise women could add value. Households with two incomes have also added to house prices.

It's ironic that so many houses are unaffordable without two incomes, yet we live in a society that readily accepts single living. I'm not suggesting both sexes and both parents shouldn't work. But there are consequences. My outlook has certainly changed since I studied law when I expected to change the world while still wearing a bra. Now I'll happily retire when the time comes and watch cricket in my dressing gown.

22 August 2021

Mr M and I are watching a Bill Bailey sketch about him going for a massage. The masseuse took a deep breath when she saw him, which he took to be a positive reflection on his manhood. He quickly felt small when told that he'd mistaken his disposable pants for a hairnet. Hubby and I roar with laughter, not only because it was funny, but because we both know I'd made the same mistake sixteen years ago.

I'd gone for my biennial health check and one of the results necessitated a minor procedure to avoid a much more serious illness that could become untreatable. I was panic-stricken as it was only eight days before I was temporarily leaving work to travel round South America for four months. Not only would my health cover be suspended but I didn't want to postpone the treatment until after my return.

"Don't worry, we've got you booked into theatre on Tuesday," announced the friendly doctor.

Well, it was me that put on a show for the nurses and porter. I'd been left alone to change out of my clothes into the hospital gown. I was sitting on the edge of the bed when the nurse returned and immediately burst out laughing. I thought that was unnecessary given the garment was hospital issue. It wasn't my fault I didn't look like a catwalk model.

"What have you got on your head?"

"The hairnet!"

"That's not a hairnet. They're your disposable knickers," countered the nurse, as she shouted down the corridor inviting all the hospital staff to come and have a look and a guffaw.

"What did you think the leg holes were for?"

"My ears, obviously. I thought it was unhygienic leaving my hair loose."

23 August 2021

Hubby took me for lunch in Oakham before we checked into our hotel for our two-night stay celebrating our fourth wedding anniversary. We don't normally go to such lengths, but in the absence of foreign holidays, decided to treat ourselves. The hotel has the longest standing Michelin star restaurant in the UK and it personalised tonight's menu with an anniversary message. I didn't have the heart to tell them they were a day early.

24 August 2021

It's four years since the best day of my life. We hired e-bikes to cycle round Rutland Water, and I never thought I'd want more padding on my backside. I felt violated. Every cyclist regardless of finishing position deserves a medal for balancing on those seats for so long.

Hubby's cousin and her husband joined us for dinner but not before we'd enjoyed some Kent sparkling wine on the terrace overlooking the immaculate hotel gardens and Rutland Water. Two nights here may cost the same as an all-inclusive week in the Canaries, and it's worth every penny.

25 August 2021

England bowled India out for seventy-eight on day one of the next test, more quickly than I can do the two loads of washing we created while away for two nights. Hubby reckoned the test match would be over in three days. I reminded him that you never know in cricket.

I told the friends we're staying with from tomorrow that my test is negative. I didn't need to qualify that I wasn't announcing I wasn't pregnant.

26 August 2021

Why does it always feel such a rush to get out of the door when we're going away for a few days? We can and should take the time to check we have what we need and haven't forgotten anything. It's a luxury those fleeing from their homes in Afghanistan don't have. Twenty years after the Taliban was overthrown, it has again taken control over most of the country, and residents hasten to escape, afraid of the rules under which they may otherwise be forced to live.

27 August 2021

We couldn't get on the intended train to Headingley from Leeds as it was rammed, and were privileged to get a table seat on the next one. Unfortunately, the guard tells us we're all on the wrong train so we all head further up the platform as directed. About ten minutes later, we're all told to reboard the original train, and this time we end up standing.

I've become so used to knowing what I am doing and when, and how to find my way around the house we've barely left in the last eighteen months, that I find the inept handling of an expected crowd of people really annoying.

28 August 2021

After yesterday's debacle at Leeds, we get the slightly

slower, but direct train from York to Headingley. Yet again, I pick the ground's entry queue with the security member that wants to know the colour of my rucksack stitching before letting me in. I hate queuing. I don't know why people say the Brits are good at queueing. Define good. It's not the queue per se that winds me up. It's the inefficiencies that keep me in it longer than is necessary, and may mean others behind me miss the first delivery.

Every time I contemplated going for a drink, a wicket fell. The resultant rush to the bar meant that there was always more than around a dozen people in front of me. After each of a few attempts to get a drink, which involved standing for a couple of minutes without moving, I abandon the bar queue as I haven't come to watch the back of the head of the person in front who is desperate for a six pound pint.

England win before lunch, so we all do what any cricket fan does in such a situation and head to the local brewery. I hope everyone in the same train carriage enjoyed our singing on the way back to York.

29 August 2021

We're back home in plenty of time to sort ourselves for our cul-de-sac barbeque. Our neighbour kindly kept the burgers I had made for it and frozen. He defrosted them in time for the party, and I made a huge feta salad. It never left the fridge.

Our friend came to join us, the first time we've seen him since his sixtieth in December 2019, and the first since his wife died. I surprised myself we didn't both end up in tears.

30 August 2021

When I descend, I find three empty mugs on the granite. I don't remember making tea for the three of us. I'm pleased my libations the night before hadn't stopped me offering some hospitality to our guest in the early hours.

I'm also thrilled the cul-de-sac fairy has tidied up, as in previous years. We're left with our barbecue, a pair of sunglasses, a grey plate, and a plastic glass. Only the barbecue is ours and we're missing a wine glass and shot glass.

31 August 2021

Everyone's belongings have been returned to their rightful owners, and I start twenty-five days on the wagon.

While watching *Vigil*, I see a sign saying trespassers will be prosecuted, and wonder who takes any notice of it.

Hubby tells me we can't watch the third episode as I wish, because we have to wait until Sunday. Who waits anymore?

Geronimo, the alpaca that has twice tested positive for bovine tuberculosis has been put down under Government order, to restrict the virus spread. Thankfully, Government's not ordered the same with those testing Covid positive.

SEPTEMBER 2021

1 September 2021

Colin Pitchfork, the first person to be convicted using DNA evidence, has been released from prison, thirty-three years after being incarcerated for raping and murdering two teenagers. I wonder where he'll go and how he'll get financial support. What happens to former prisoners?

The sheets in the spare rooms get laundered more than our own at the moment.

It's my second day on the wagon. I fancy a glass of wine.

2 September 2021

Mr M decides to be tea total with me. I appreciate his support, even if it isn't his motive.

3 September 2021

Aaargh!

4 September 2021

Our first weekend in a few without any plans, so I can pick up a scarf I left at the dry cleaner. Hubby decided to come with me so we could have a wander for Christmas gift inspiration. We didn't do any wandering, as we were wondering at the lack of precautions being taken, despite cases rising amongst the double-jabbed and increasing hospitalisations.

We came straight home.

5 September 2021

Summer's back so we've spent a few hours tidying the garden. It's never looked better despite two plants not flowering at all this year. Perhaps they needed to hibernate.

I'm now quite pleased we've had to wait for our *Vigil* fix. Waiting a week has heightened the suspense, and gives us something to look forward to on Sunday evenings.

It's a bit like waiting to open Christmas presents until the day itself. My sister and I stayed up until midnight on Christmas Eve once, with our parents' permission, and vowed never to do it again as the next day was a complete anti-climax.

6 September 2021

It's the first time I've had to stay away from home for work since pre-'vid. Our department's getting together for some training. It took me about six times as long to pack as it used to. I'd only added masks and sanitiser to my usual list. I'm obviously out of the packing habit.

I am also out of the driving habit. I'd forgotten how stressful I found it, until a lorry indicated it was pulling out, despite me being alongside. The driver ignored my horn and I only avoided a collision as there wasn't anything in the lane to my right into which I had to promptly swerve.

The back of the lorry had one of those signs asking how it was being driven. I rang one of those numbers once. My call was answered by the driver who gave me verbal abuse, so I didn't bother sharing my thoughts this time.

7 September 2021

I'm really glad I wasn't drinking last night. There are some grey faces at breakfast and some noticeable absences.

8 September 2021

Groundhog Day

I'm really glad I wasn't drinking last night. There are some grey faces at breakfast and some noticeable absences.

18:00

It's great to be home again and my darling SB has totally surprised me. He's had a selfie of us on our recent wedding anniversary enlarged and printed on a framed canvas. It's hanging in Queen corner. Not only does Hubby not like lots of photos around the house, he's also never keen on any of him. Maybe I should go away more often.

I can hear him in chuntering in the living room. He's struggling to get the rugby stream to work. He stops moaning when I tell him the game's on tomorrow.

9 September 2021

I am a new knackered. Evidently being surrounded by, and talking with, forty-five colleagues has become very tiring as I'm not used to processing all the body language while trying to respect some social distance.

10 September 2021

My best friend thinks she's getting old because she has bought a new pillow and some non-wired bras. I remind her that I wash our pillows annually and buying new ones is a sign of common sense, not age. I also ask how on earth she can wear a bra that isn't under-wired without looking like she's hiding oranges in stockings under her tops.

11 September 2021

It's twenty years since the date most people of my generation will forever remember where they were. The twin towers in New York fell that day after planes flew into them in a terrorist attack by Al Qaeda.

Today may forever be etched on the next generation's minds for a different reason. Emma Radacanu became the first British woman to win a major singles title since Virginia Wade at Wimbledon in 1977, and the first ever qualifier to reach and win a major singles final. Not only did both of today's finalists play remarkable tennis, but they also spoke afterwards with dignity, gratitude, and poise.

12 September 2021

It's thirteen years since we cremated Grandma, and it would have been my grandparents' wedding anniversary. Granny Dingo said her life began when she married Gramps, and so our family felt it fitting to have her funeral on the same date.

Hubby and I are going to meet his sister and husband for brunch so I can't answer the incoming video call from my sister. She sends me a video later on, proving my suspicion that she was with our folks when she tried calling me. In the video, Mum and Dad are holding onto each other tightly, while standing outside their front door. I can't decide if Mum's worried Dad may run off with a passer-by, or whether she's had a gin and Dad's holding her up. Mum sends me a loving message saying how good it is to see me, then promptly corrects that false statement, before turning to Dad.

"I'm busy," he says, releasing Mum and scurrying indoors. Mum doesn't fall over so can't have had a gin.

13 September 2021

I became disproportionately excited when I found some washing machine cleaner in the utility room. I'd forgotten we bought it ages ago when we used to go into supermarkets. We'd taken a short cut down the aisle with the mono-slippers and clothing de-fuzz shavers, when we spotted it and thought we'd better get some. I think we forgot what we'd gone in for.

14 September 2021

Why can't I get dressed without deodorant marks covering my clothes?

I'd barely recovered from yesterday's excitement generated from cleaning the washing machine, when the new bottle shelf for our fridge arrived. I cracked the original before it had even needed cleaning and it's been annoying us both for the last thirty months.

I decided to buy another, so searched the manufacturer's website. The product I selected prompted me for more information, and I was invited to an online chat function. I typed my request and hit send.

"We're sorry that our chat function is closed today. Please try again."

I searched for the product number and found another website that only needed my credit card and delivery details. The fridge manufacturer I tried first lost a sale because it claimed to need more information from me, presumably so it could try to sell me more products.

15 September 2021

I went for a haircut. All the stylists wore masks although didn't insist I did. I did. My stylist was coughing and spluttering behind his and assured me it was just a cold. He justified coming to work on the basis it didn't let his clients down.

I wonder if it will become unacceptable for employees to attend a communal place of work if they're displaying potentially contagious symptoms. Our nation seems to be divided into two: those that take any opportunity not to work, and those that would drag themselves in on stumps if their limbs had been blown off, while declaring, "It's just a bit of blood!"

16 September 2021

Our wonderful nephew is ten. Amidst all the fear that our children will suffer for years to come, I'm thankful he is happy and seems high on life. I wonder how many of our children's fears are absorbed from mis-placed concern amongst adults.

I also wonder while watching the footy, how many will be named Patson, after Leicester City's new Zambian signing, Patson Daka. I told Hubby that lots of newborns have been christened Dua, after the singer Dua Lipa.

"How ridiculous," he snorts.

"That's her real name!"

It reminds me that Rolls Royce once changed the planned name for the Silver Shadow. The luxury automobile manufacturer abandoned the name Silver Mist when someone noted that mist meant manure, and possibly worse, in German.

If only Newcastle University hadn't embarrassed itself when it tried, in 2013, to patent the names Central University upon Tyne and the Civil University of North Tyneside. Rumour has it, the faux pas was only spotted when the acronym-adorned stationery came back from the printer.

17 September 2021

Hubby went off to golf wishing me a productive day. A system outage meant I couldn't do what I had planned, so I took the opportunity to do other tasks that usually get pushed down the priority list, sometimes for months.

When Mr M returned, I told him that my day had been productive, recognising that doing something other than what I had planned doesn't mean it wasn't. I suppose if I had left matters to the last minute, I may have felt less calm, so am grateful I have been sufficiently organised.

The two reversible ponchos I ordered have arrived. The care label says to wash them inside out!

18 September 2021

I take a lateral flow test as we're meeting friends to go to our first live rugby match since pre-'vid. Tigers gave me plenty of reasons to jump up and down and my impending black eyes are two reasons I should have kept my feet planted on the terraces we have missed gracing.

Perhaps unexpectedly, the Tigers defeated last year's runners-up, causing some neutrals to rush for the betting apps before the odds shorten too much. We're twenty-five to one to win the Premiership and I wonder if it's worth a fiver. Which decision would I regret more?

I thought I was getting used to my forgetfulness, but astounded myself when we got home by forgetting to get the cash out of my purse for which I had gone upstairs. In a tenuous attempt to find a positive, I mentally noted the additional sixty-two steps I had to take towards the recommended daily total of ten thousand, so I could get the money to pay for our takeaway.

19 September 2021

Yesterday's fresh air and Tigger-like terrace jumping must have worn me out as I slept until the cup of tea Hubby had placed by our bed was cold. My tiredness was equally likely to have been because my brain didn't switch off until about 01:00, thinking about all the weekends away, and a 2023 hen do I am in the throes of planning.

Mr M was reading the paper chuntering something I misheard. I asked if sign language was globally consistent. If so, why don't we teach that in schools so we can communicate across the globe? He believes there are different sign languages, so deaf people need to learn multiple signals for the same word, depending on the nationality of the person with whom they're communicating. As if the deaf don't have enough barriers to being able to converse.

One of last night's *Strictly* contestants is deaf. She had a person signing for her so she could understand everything. How will her partner teach her to dance to a beat she cannot hear? In her own words, they'll find a way. If the group dance performance is indicative, they already have.

I'm embarrassed at how easily I have sometimes been defeated in life, when I am able-bodied and of sound mind. My friends sometime question the latter, which reminds me I must do my subconscious bias training at work.

20 September 2021

My plans are all coming together. It's like mixing cake ingredients, then watching with anticipation as the cake rises in the oven. My planning reward won't be a delicious cake, but will hopefully be enjoyable times with appreciative friends.

21 September 2021

Kwasi Kwarteng, the Secretary of State for Business, Energy, and Industrial Strategy, has announced loans for energy companies, struggling with recent price hikes. I had wondered about whom a friend was talking, when she'd called him Quasi Quango, and also whether that would be deemed insulting or offensive. If not now, it may be deemed so in ten years and she'll have to delete all her social media posts that included it.

22 September 2021

I barely dare mention the C word in our house but I am thinking ahead to Christmas. And compared to the other C words, this one has to be preferable.

We refused to be disheartened last year when we couldn't host or see family as usual. We didn't think it was sensible to take advantage of the reduced restrictions, favouring lunch for the two of us instead. Hubby planned an Italian menu which didn't get eaten until Boxing Day as we were both ill. I managed to eat three slices of mozzarella and some ice-cream on Christmas Day. I also stuck to the Italian theme as I turned various shades of red, green, and white, as I overheated, and then felt queasy before the blood drained from my face.

The law says I could have recovered the annual leave I had taken after Christmas last year, as I had been ill during it. But I had already been absent due to illness before that holiday, and I didn't think taking more time as sick leave was helpful.

I can't believe that was around nine months ago. Life seems to be zipping by faster than a four-year-old ski-ing past me on the slopes, while the pandemic simultaneously drags on.

23 September 2021

As the headlines report more energy companies entering insolvency, a friend tells me his wife may have had her unique wedding ring stolen from her bedside in South Africa.

I'm so upset for her. I was brought up to respect other people's property, and certainly not to steal it.

I remember when I was around twelve, I'd been looking at some tape to wrap presents with. It was adorned with Santas and snowmen. When I left the shop and put my hands in my pockets, I found two rolls of tape for which I hadn't paid. I immediately returned to the store to pay. I was shaking with fear that I'd be caught outside the shop, and not be able to convince any adult that I'd unwittingly put them in my pocket.

Stealing the show, or stealing glances of someone famous may be acceptable. Stealing from someone else surely isn't!

24 September 2021

I'm going to visit friends in Woking tomorrow. I've done a list of where I need to be, by when, and at what time I need to leave each. I don't remember doing this pre-'vid.

****

What is the point of AutoSave if not to prevent data loss after a computer crash?

The entries that follow up to and including 30 October 2021 have been reconstructed on 15 November 2021, largely from memory, following a computer crash and AutoSave fail.

****

25 September 2021

It's been a great day visiting friends. I'd forgotten how expensive leaving the house is. If I added up the cost of the return fuel, afternoon gin at the distillery, hotel, meal, drinks, and extortionate parking, it would total around two hundred pounds. It would have been more if I hadn't used points for the hotel, or vouchers for the food. It's been worth every penny.

26 September 2021

I'm glad to be home with Hubby.

29 September 2021

We're watching a series about a popular hirsute couple of gentleman that tour the country on two wheels. Tonight's show is based on the doorstep of where I was born, and where we're shortly spending a weekend with two other couples we met in Sri Lanka.
It rivals Sri Lanka's beauty and I feel guilty that I forget how stunning it is.

30 September 2021

I joined the MenoPAUSE group at work. I feel old.
Hubby trapped his scrotum just as the radio played *We're caught in a trap*. I was more amused than him.
Nicolas Sarkozy has been sentenced to a year in prison for illegally funding his unsuccessful 2012 re-election campaign. In March, he received a custodial sentence for corruption, and remains free pending his appeal. He can serve his time at home

with an electric bracelet, and some may be curious to know why he's not behind bars.

OCTOBER 2021

1 October 2021

I've just watched a police interview with Wayne Couzens, himself a policeman, arrested under suspicion of kidnap. He claims he was being threatened by a gang or similar over his financial issues. He says his family were at risk and so he hadn't any choice but to give the gang someone else.

It seems money could indeed be the root of evil. If guilty of murder, Mr Couzens faces a whole-life order, and will be one of around sixty serving the same, never eligible for release.

3 October 2021

It would be easier to crack a safe than book to see James Bond.

Where do you want to sit?
What food do you want?
What drink do you want?
What's your email address?
What's your credit card number?
What is your inside leg measurement?*

*They didn't ask that.

I couldn't complete my booking request as the system needed to send a one-time passcode, and didn't have my phone number. Why didn't it ask for that, and why won't it let me add it now?

4 October 2021

My sister-in-law has featured on TV and reminds us that not everyone will be able to fully enjoy freedom when the rules are entirely relaxed. She is vulnerable and isolating again and can only meet outdoors with people who have had both vaccines.

Gandhi said, "The true measure of any society can be found in how it treats its most vulnerable members."

5 October 2021

I'm organising numerous events and agreeing to more will become stressful. Freedom shouldn't bring more work than I feel I can cope with. I said I wouldn't go back to a new normal and would go back to better instead! I must decline any future requests until I have finished organising the events to which I have already given my commitment.

7 October 2021

I've made a quiche and fish pie to take with us tomorrow for a long weekend with two other couples we met almost ten years ago in Sri Lanka. I should have bought the shortbread biscuits like a normal person, instead of staying up until 23:30 to make them.

8 October 2021

The lodge has everything we could want, nestled in the Forest of Bowland with nothing in sight expect trees and ducks.

We enjoyed the fish pie and Hubby's meatballs (not together), and I'm glad I made biscuits.

Our friend has brought *Outburst*. Each team has to guess as many of ten answers to different topics. She asks us to name things that go up. We haven't stopped laughing from the first answer given, when she realises she misread it. She should have asked for things that group. It doesn't change our answer, and leaves us contemplating if it's groups of dicks that are still spreading this disease. There's been over thirty thousand new cases and one hundred and twenty-seven deaths.

9 October 2021

The hot tub is very welcome after our ten-mile yomp, before our evening game.

None of us realised how long it would take to play *Monopoly* with six of us. I had planned to have an earlier second night, as we'd stayed up on our first until around 02:00, and I needed more sleep.

But playing *Monopoly* brought happy memories of playing it in my maternal grandparents' caravan, when my sister and I were children. I was always the boat and my sister was the boot.

I've bought Sis a crystal boot Christmas tree decoration. Last year I sent her an angel and I sent Mum a crystal heart. I'd included a note saying that although we wouldn't be together at Christmas, my heart was always with her. This year I have bought Mum an angel, and unlike last year, I shall be able to hand deliver it when we meet for lunch at the end of the month.

Unfortunately, Hubby woke me at 01:05 shouting that something had bitten him. He'd been stung by one of the drowsy wasps we thought must be living in the stone walls, one of which had fallen into our bed. His finger swelled to the size of a Cumberland sausage before I could get a cold compress on it.

10 October 2021

Mr M's finger has gone down and he no longer feels like he's being stabbed with a red hot poker.

We played *Balderdash*, a game in which players make up answers to various topics including names and events. All the answers and the real one are read out. Each player takes turn to guess which is real. Points are awarded to players for correct answers, and also if their bluff is offered by another player as the correct answer.

Some players try to double bluff by suggesting their own bluff is the real answer, hoping that subsequent players may be persuaded to say the same, thus giving points to the double-bluffer. As one of our friends found out, suggesting your own bluff is the correct answer, isn't a sensible tactic if you're the last of the players to guess.

11 October 2021

We had coffee with my folks as they live near to where we were staying. It never seems long enough. It could never be long enough.

12 October 2021

A colleague sends me pictures of her new purse and bag, which she's bought with the reward voucher for which I had nominated her. I'm so pleased for her, not least as I hadn't known she'd been using a ripped purse for the last year as she couldn't afford another.

13 October 2021

My friend messaged to say my thank you card had arrived. She said she knew it was from me before she'd even read it, as I am the only person to send written thanks. She said it means so much more than a text, and I should never stop sending them.

My parents used to make my sister and me write thanks for any gifts we received as children. I wanted to thank our friends for a lovely weekend, so sent them all a note.

14 October 2021

I'm so excited that Hubby and I will see a comedian tomorrow that we had originally booked to see in February 2020.

15 October 2021

He was hilarious. While at the comedy, my sister left me a message asking if I fancy a video call at the weekend. This rare request and the sentiment of it makes my bottom lip wobble.

Tomorrow is a year since my friend died.

I crash into tears during our journey home.

16 October 2021

I've got to feed the neighbours' cat for the next six days. Why did I volunteer? I tend to set house alarms off, and the cat's so old, it may die on my watch, and I would be mortified.

17 October 2021

The cat immediately appeared as I arrived. Phew.

18 October 2021

Next week I have to go to Glasgow for work. It's the first time I won't be doing client work from home since March 2020. It feels like the worst timing. There's been around fifty thousand new cases although daily deaths remain below one hundred.

But there'll be road closures, train strikes and heightened security in Glasgow because of COP26. It's the twenty-sixth Conference of the Parties to the United Nations Framework Convention on Climate Change. It aims to agree actions that will keep global warming below one and a half degrees centigrade.

Am I more likely to catch the virus, or be accosted by someone protesting that I have flown, when we're trying to reduce emissions?

19 October 2021

Where is the moggy? OMG. What if it's been runover?

20 October 2021

The cat's alive. Phew.

The scientists are trying to explain that more of us may stay that way if we had our booster jab. Less than half of those entitled have had it.

21 October 2021

I'll miss feeding that cat.

22 October 2021

Our neighbour has just brought a magnum of red round for feeding the pet. It would have been cheaper to put it in the cattery. I must volunteer again.

23 October 2021

People are standing in the town centre with placards saying children are fifty times more likely to die from the vaccine than from the virus. I have no idea what statistics support their statement. I'm just glad I don't have to make the decision.

My parents, not unreasonably, declined the offer of a whooping cough vaccine for me when it was relatively new and the potential side effects couldn't be fully known. I contracted whooping cough when I was around four and was very ill. Poor Mum had to regularly change my bedsheets. Dad would cuddle me on the sofa as he watched Match of the Day. I'm sure that's where my love of the game started.

24 October 2021

It feels like I have spent my whole Sunday getting ready for work next week.

25 October 2021

I've arrived safely at the hotel and am pleasantly surprised that more of its facilities are open than the website suggested. Perhaps that's a silver lining of next week's conference.

27 October 2021

The restaurant staff recognise me after my two previous bookings. I'd normally try different places, but this feels safe and non-judgmental of a single female. The staff are great although I have exceeded my expense budget most nights. It's costing me money to work!

Bond was awesome but I miss intervals. I'll have to see it again as I missed a bit to go for a pee.

28 October 2021

I've been looking forward to tonight and not only as it's the last before I return home. I'm going to see a live stream of the Rocky Horror Picture Show that's on in a London theatre. Hubby can't comprehend why grown men dress in stockings and basques to watch.

29 October 2021

I'm home by around 09:30 after getting up at 04:00 to catch my flight. As we disembarked, the staff asked us to respect people's space and distance. I wondered what the point was when we were all subsequently crammed like sardines into a transfer bus.

When Hubby gets back from golf, he tells me he's struggled without me this week, but didn't want to tell me over the phone.

30 October 2021

Hubby and I agree what we're going to eat next week. I tell him we're totally psychopathic. He proves my point by telling me I mean telepathic.

31 October 2021

We met my parents, and sister and family for lunch to celebrate Mum's birthday. We wondered if it really was Mum when she ordered a burger. She doesn't like burgers. We've never seen her eat one. She left the bread and ate the meat!

As her gift, we paid for Mum and Dad to stay the night, partly so Dad doesn't have to drive fifty miles home in the dark.

We used to drive three-hundred-and-twenty-mile round trips to have lunch with family, at restaurants further north than they lived. Our journey home invariably ended up in a row from tiredness, after which I'd fall asleep while poor Hubby fought to stay awake while driving. It's bliss to have found somewhere equidistant between my sister and us, that we all enjoyed.

We were home in time to watch a film which is traditional at this time of year and that I'd never seen. I wonder if poltergeists have stolen my mum and replaced her with a Maccie D or Burger King fan.

NOVEMBER 2021

1 November 2021

I was able to prepare dinner during my lunch break. It's one of the benefits of working from home. Some people find it hard to focus when not in an office. I'm the opposite and have always got through a lot more work without the distractions of ringing phones, or various people chatting.

Some people who've never done it don't trust those that do. While working away once, a friend messaged me asking if I was working from home that day. He wanted me to take him that afternoon to collect his new car from the garage about forty miles away. As it happened, I wasn't at home, but would still have declined on the basis that I was working. The clue is in the title.

3 November 2021

Mum's birthday

I'm making treacle toffee to take to friends' on Saturday. Who has cream of tartar in their cupboards? It comes in a quantity twenty-four times my recipe requirement. A best before end date of 2023 isn't long enough.

I've got bored holding the thermometer in the pan to see if the mixture has reached the essential cracking point. The thermometer nearly split while resting on the side of the pan. I think bits of the black plastic top may have melted into the treacle.

The recipe says it takes about thirty minutes. I've been

standing here for ninety and have run out of wine. Being creative is supposed to help your mental well-being. I think my brain has dissolved. The two-tone colour of the pan contents suggest the sugar has separated from the rest of the ingredients, and now the sodding thermometer battery isn't working.

Some of the treacle toffee-making videos I have watched have recipes that take the time of a gnat's fart. I've been standing for almost two hours getting ever nearer to death. It's bed-time. The thermometer has reincarnated and at least one part of the mix is the correct temperature. That'll do. It'll take until Saturday to cool down, and can heat the house while doing so.

4 November 2021

I have found out why yesterday's coffee had coagulated slush in the bottom of the mug and tasted bitter. The milk was off! I had two cups of it yesterday and thought the strange flavour was from some new beans.

5 November 2021

I spent most of the afternoon typing through tears contemplating not going to the evening's rugby match. Our friend wasn't going to come either, as she had a packed weekend and was feeling a little stressed. Thankfully we both went and our company was just what we each needed. The victory helped too.

6 November 2021

Tonight will be guaranteed fun. Hubby and I have told ourselves we will not stay up until 04:00 as often happens with these friends.

After the main course I notice I've had my knickers on inside out all day. I have déjà vu.

I'm not sure how we then ended up talking about the hernia test commonly known as the cough and drop. I also don't know why I kept calling it the cough and cup.

My treacle toffee looked delicious, initially. But it mustn't have uniformly reached the vital cracking point temperature that keeps it solid, and after slowly melting on the plate, it looked like a burst implant!

We went to bed at 03:00.

7 November 2021

Our breathalyser says we are both negative, thanks to some very disciplined pacing with our drinks. I forgot to pack clean underwear. Is it better than to turn a pair inside out than go commando?

On the way home, I remember that we'd been talking about classic films I'd never seen. I ask Hubby if we should watch *Butch Kennedy and the Sundance Kid,* so I'm not the only one of us who hasn't seen it.

"Don't worry, babe. You're definitely not the only one who hasn't seen that!"

8 November 2021

I've put the treacle sludge in the bin, read the Sunday paper, done yoga, prepared for the third interview in a series of four, and had a bath. It's a perfect start to the next week off.

9 November 2021

My week off work feels like work. It's taken an hour and a half to complete an ongoing interview process.

10 November 2021

I've finished the interview process. I was glad the three remaining tests were timed, or I may have spent the rest of my holiday figuring out the correct answers to the logic tests.

I booked a long weekend in Norwich in May 2022, for the six of us that recently went to the Forest of Bowland.

I told Hubby I am not arranging anything else for a while.

"That's what you said after the last time!"

I have booked weekends in Bath in February and in Exeter in March, both to watch rugby. From Exeter we're going to Cornwall for my birthday and will catch up with some friends while there. After Norfolk with friends in May, my sister, her fiancé, and we, will celebrate her fiftieth at Hambleton Hall in July as our birthday gift. We've also booked to go to Norwich in August and are taking our folks as Dad's eightieth gift and Mum's seventy-fifth. We're hoping to see Dad's Aunt with whom he has started to enjoy a relationship over the last few years, after decades without much contact, if any.

I'm organising sixteen hens for a long weekend in April 2023. I'm thankful I can operate a spreadsheet to keep track of all the payments, deposits, and money that others owe me.

I've had to scavenge the house for enough change to be able to buy dinner at the chippy. I was musing how ridiculously cheap chips were, when I realised while walking back home that I'd forgotten to order my own food. I couldn't be bothered to go back and queue again while surrounded by maskless people. I shared Hubby's large chips and smothered them in cheese and gravy. It sounds gross but is delicious, much like the French dish, poutine.

11 November 2021

I'm having lunch with a former boss. What do people wear to have lunch out? We're going to a restaurant where a friend, sadly no longer with us, first explained my profession to me around twenty-three years ago.

How is it possible that my first four choices of footwear all need repairs?

Mr M messaged me while I was doing yoga upstairs during his online training in the study. He asked me if I can remember the legal doctrine that says a plaintiff will be unable to pursue legal relief if it arises in connection with their own tortious act.

Ex turpi causa non oritur actio meaning, *no action arises from deceit.*

It reminds me of a case study a lawyer once told me. An insolvency practitioner was trying to sell an empty property owned by a company that had gone into receivership. The receiver recognised the injury risk to the public as the property was in poor repair. He used funds from other company asset sales, to pay for fences and signs warning trespassers of the dangers, and telling people to keep out or face prosecution.

A boy of about twelve climbed over the six-foot fence and onto the property roof. He fell through and broke his arm. His mum sued. Mine might have been tempted to clip my ears, smack my bum, and send me to bed without dinner, as punishment for my wrong-doing.

The property insurer was confident it could defend the boy's claim. The child could read and knew trespassing was wrong. The judge said the insolvency practitioner had done almost everything he could to protect the public, but evidently hadn't done enough. He found in favour of the boy that broke the law. It may feel as if the only arse being spanked that day was the law itself.

It's sixty-eight quid for my shoe repairs. I have forgotten the cost of living.

I finally watched *Butch Cassidy and the Sundance Kid.*

12 November 2021

Our friendly post lady took the letter she saw me with, to save me the trouble of walking to the box.

I got home and remembered I'd intended checking the church notices en route to the post box, so went back out again.

Hubby's not working today and isn't playing golf either so we can go to the cinema and have dinner out on the last working day of my week off.

The film proved I don't understand sci-fi despite reading the synopsis before watching it.

After the cinema, the waitress remembered us and immediately told us they didn't have my preferred wine. I hope she remembered us because we are always polite and tip well. We always use supermarket vouchers to pay for the food at this Italian restaurant under some sort of partnership agreement. Every little helps.

We also always tip on what would have been the full meal bill, and check with the waitress if she gets tips paid on card. My niece has recently left a job where the boss was keeping her tips. She was known as one of his best waitresses. What a false economy it must have been. I'm pleased she left. It seems some employers think that loyal staff won't leave.

Britney has also left her father's conservatorship after thirteen years. The court has terminated the legal arrangement, with his consent.

14 November 2021

Remembrance Day

I got home from my annual trip to church and noticed my socks were holey.

The vicar had spoken about needing younger people to help us when our computers don't work. I felt prematurely smug that I have mastered switching mine on and off, and that it has an AutoSave function.

After I got home, due to my computer crashing, and an AutoSave fail, I haven't achieved what I had planned to during my week off. I can only hope it's not another serious virus. It's perhaps unfortunate that switching the world off and on again isn't an option.

15 November 2021

Why don't computers and printers work on the first day after annual leave?

16 November 2021

We need to switch off racism. Cricket's being accused of being institutionally racist with stories of Muslims being forced to drink wine, and being called by different names than their own.

We all know people that say they're not racist and follow that statement with "but". Unless we all take responsibility to question people's behaviours, it will take too long to stamp out. Children aren't born racist, so they must learn it. Doesn't racism drive the division and war that racists fear?

17 November 2021

I used a packet chilli mix for the evening meal, instead of making it from scratch.

"Hubby, am I allowed to say I prefer it to the recipe I usually follow?"

"So do I."

"Really? I only make that recipe as I thought you liked it more than the packet mix."

"You silly moo!"

I think of all the hours I have spent grinding spices and chopping onions when I could have torn a packet open. Hubby's grateful I stay calm, unlike a thirty-six-year-old woman who's been jailed for stabbing her spouse, because he didn't support her in an argument.

18 November 2021

Hubby's excitement about our new roasting tin is palpable and now he's sending me pictures of kettles he likes! He asks me if I think he is getting old.

19 November 2021

Colin Pitchfork has been sent back to a closed prison for breaching his licence conditions, two months after his release following a thirty-three year incarceration for murdering two teenage girls. Staff at the hostel where he was staying were becoming concerned at his behaviour, although there's no evidence of another offence. Nevertheless, it seems he may never be allowed out again.

I wonder why he learnt braille in jail and hope it isn't to prey on those that can't recognise him. Maybe it's because he thinks only the sightless would ever be friends with him. He may never get chance to use it.

Alex Hales has apologised for causing offence when he wore black makeup to a party twelve years ago to which he went dressed as his favourite musician, Tupac. I'm all for stamping out racism and offensive behaviour.

I've read some commentary asking if we are saying that you can't emulate your heroes if you're white, and you want to go to a fancy dress party as your idol who is black. Some believe recognising talent, no matter what the person's colour, would only help the cause to stop the division. They are questioning if we can't recognise talent unless we're the same colour.

I wonder if Dolly Parton concert attendees will stop putting footballs down their tops and donning wigs. Dolly admits to faking many of her attributes, openly stating it costs a lot of money to look that cheap. I wonder if she is offended when her fans mimic her appearance while paying to listen to her. Do those who go to a party dressed as Elvis towards the end of his career risk being called fattist, as well as fattest?

20 November 2021

England beat the World Rugby Union Champions, South Africa by one point with a late penalty which was ironic, given how many penalties we conceded compared to them.

Manchester United's manager has been sacked after a crushing defeat to Watford yesterday. There can't be many careers where being sacked still results in a massive pay packet.

21 November 2021

I've been reading about HOGO, the hassle of going out, and recognise myself, as I start worrying about getting flowers for today's Sunday lunch with friends. I've been so happy working at home, cleaning our home, entertaining at home. It's our turn to go to our friends' and I really need to snap out of my lethargy. I need to get out more.

Why does everyone feel obligated to take flowers when they go to someone's house for lunch? Hubby dismisses my suggestion to buy some locally. He hasn't even seen them and I thought they looked beautiful when I went past the shop yesterday.

He drove to the out of town shopping park, and I thought I saw some lovely flowers outside the store. Hubby dropped me at the other side and directed me indoors.

"Through there and turn left and you'll find them."

I ended up exiting the store at the other side, having walked round at least half of it in vain, by which time we'd be late if I carried on looking.

When I got back in the car and explained to his quizzical face, he told me I was supposed to have looked to my right once I'd turned left.

"That's not what you told me."

Silently fuming that my initial plan to support the local shops would have meant we didn't turn up empty handed, I was thankful we did have a couple of bottles of wine with us.

We were right on time and easily passed almost five hours, some of which was spent watching our friend try to light candles by reusing matches. The dog's silent but deadly smells told us all he needed a walk and I was glad we'd blown out the naked flames.

We got home and I ordered, for direct delivery to our friends, a contraption with which to safely light candles.

22 November 2021

I proudly told Hubby when he returned from golf that I had walked a little today.

"Where did you go?"

"To the post box."

Kevin Sinfield is travelling one hundred and one miles on foot in twenty-four hours from this morning. Just before 09:00, he will leave Welford Road, the home of Leicester Tigers, where he is a defence coach. He hopes to arrive around the same time tomorrow at Headingley, home of the Rugby League team for which he played for eighteen years.

He's already raised three times his target to help fund Motor Neurone Disease research and facilities. His close friend and former teammate at Leeds was diagnosed in 2019. It affects the brain and nerves and eventually stops muscles functioning. When Stephen Hawking died in 2018 he'd been communicating through a speech-generating machine, using his only working muscle in his cheek to operate it.

Kevin has to cover seven kilometres every hour. He's hoping Rob Burrow will be well enough to meet him at the finish. When the route was calculated, it was one mile more than his plan. It wasn't a surprise people started saying he'll be going the extra mile, again. He raised over two and a half million pounds in December 2020 when he ran seven marathons in seven days, the common number being what Rob wore on his back while playing rugby.

I've no doubt Kevin will get there in time. Conversely, I am nervous that gifts posted to my Australian godsons, may not arrive in time, even if ordered from an Australian online store for direct delivery. Postal systems all over are encountering various disruptions, so I asked my friends to buy for their three sons. They kindly agreed and I need to send a cheque to my uni friend's mother, so she can give the money to him next time she goes over there. She's regularly visited Adelaide since her son emigrated, and doing this saves me the exchange and transaction fees. I have her bank details but she'd prefer a cheque. I know my friend sent me her new address some time ago. I have checked texts, WhatsApp, messenger, email, comments beneath photos in our dedicated album, my phone contacts, and my address book, all in vain.

23 November 2021

Our friend that hosted us on Sunday for lunch, messaged thanking us for the candle lighter she loved. I'd sent one in her favourite colour.

"Just get the normal one," Hubby had said. I ignored him and got the one I thought that was better suited for a woman that announced on our arrival that she loved the pink colour of my poncho. I feel better that we didn't take flowers.

Apparently Colin Pitchfork had been approaching young women near the hostel where he was staying. Hubby says he should never have been let out for what he did. Many would agree although it seems the licence conditions have prevented any further criminality. Would it ever be possible to reintegrate after a third of a century in jail?

24 November 2021

It's been thirty years since Freddie died, aged forty-five. He continues to be recognisable without mentioning his surname. His death certainly raised awareness and increased the donations to fund research into finding treatments for HIV and AIDS.

I was at my friend's when his death was announced. I started to cry, and her teenage brother said I was soft as he deserved it. It's my first memory of such homophobia from someone that age. Was he driven by misunderstanding, or fear, or neither?

Despite any fear of the potential or actual risks, thirty-one migrants have tried to reach the UK from Calais, and died. It's the worst migrant disaster in the English Channel on record.

NASA has sent a rocket to smash an asteroid.

Kevin Sinfield has raised around £1.5 million.

I have spent twenty-five minutes putting six hundred tea bags into takeaway containers. They stack neatly in the cupboard where the large bag in which they were originally packed wouldn't have fit. I was so tired afterwards, I thought it was bedtime when it was only 20:30.

25 November 2021

What is wrong with people? A twelve-year-old girl has been fatally stabbed after an argument, following which four teenage boys have been arrested for murder.

27 November 2021

We've been listening to Jon Richardson's podcast. He was talking about lowering his junk into a hot bubble bath as a form of male contraceptive. I wondered how on earth dousing broken electrical items and other scrap would help. Hubby explained the alternative meaning which made more sense. Some may think they look uglier than, without the cuteness of, a pug, but it still seems harsh to refer to men's reproductive organs as junk!

28 November 2021

V & D day

Just when I thought I'd manage the whole calendar year without a day's illness, a bug rudely kept me awake most of the night.

29 November 2021

I feel blessed to have clean water to drink, or I may have been even more ill, more dehydrated, and more tired. It can feel like an imprisonment when illness strikes, and I wonder what Ghislaine Maxwell's conditions are like. Her trial starts in the USA today. Prosecutors allege she preyed on, and groomed young girls for the convicted paedophile, Jeffrey Epstein to abuse. She was arrested and jailed last year pending trial, after which she could be sentenced to several decades behind bars.

Why does it seem worse to me when women are guilty of such offences? Is it because, even as a childless woman myself, I expect women to have some maternal or nurturing instincts? Rather than wanting to protect children, Maxwell is accused of serving them up for sexual abuse. She has pleaded not guilty to eight charges. Her defence lawyer claims she stands accused of crimes committed by Epstein. He can't be tried for them following his suicide on 10 August 2019 while in prison pending his trial.

It all reminds me of being approached while I walked in the Czech Republic in the Summer of 1993. The country had only recently formed when it split from what we now call Slovakia. I was interrailing with three uni friends and for some forgotten reason, I was unusually out on my own. The summer heat and limited backpacker's wardrobe dictated I wore cycling shorts and a crop top.

As I strolled alongside a road, a sleek, dark vehicle slowed down to keep pace alongside me, and the nearest back electric window descended. I could see a woman, possibly in her thirties although the heavy makeup made it hard to tell. She was sitting next to a mute and barely visible gentleman. She smiled as she invited my absent friends and me for free drinks that evening in their nightclub. As I read the address on the business card she'd handed me, the car sped off.

We never went to the night club. I've wondered more than once what could have become of us, and am glad that I don't know. I suspect the seemingly generous offer was too good to be true.

I also wonder how long Ms Maxwell's trial will take. The trial of O.J. Simpson spanned eleven months. He was tried for the murders of his ex-wife Nicole Brown Simpson and her friend Ronald Goldman. They were stabbed to death outside Brown's condominium in the Brentwood neighbourhood of Los Angeles on 12 June 1994. The ensuing trial may be the most publicised in history. Jurors came and went, some even tried to escape their own incarceration. Only four of the original jurors remained on the final panel. In total they were sequestered for two hundred and sixty-five days.

Sequestration is rare. The jury's isolation is to prevent their accidental or deliberate exposure to outside information or influence that wouldn't be admissible in court. The jury is ordinarily kept in a hotel without access to newspapers, television, or the internet. They have limited contact with each other.

It's becoming less common partly due to the expense, and also the concerns about the impact on the jury members. The judge in the O.J. trial recognised that jurors were struggling to cope while isolated, and so allowed them to see their families after a while. It sounds too familiar.

The defence team of several lawyers, including one of the Kardashian family, was able to convince the jury that there was reasonable doubt concerning the DNA evidence, a relatively new form of evidence. The defence claimed a blood sample had been mishandled by lab technicians and scientists, and questioned the circumstances of other court exhibits. The team also alleged other misconduct by the Los Angeles Police Department, including systemic racism and incompetence.

The trial has its own Wikipedia page and has spawned numerous books by various authors including prosecutors, and police officers. There's also been a series in which John Travolta played one of the defence lawyers, Robert Shapiro.

After the trial, Goldman's father filed a civil suit against O.J. On 4 February 1997, partly thanks to a lower burden of proof in civil trials, the jury unanimously found Simpson responsible for the deaths of both victims and awarded compensatory and punitive damages totalling thirty-three and a half million dollars. Around three years later, Simpson left California for Florida, one of the few states where personal assets such as homes and pensions cannot be seized to cover liabilities that were incurred in other states. Apparently, the Goldman family has only been paid about one percent of the award.

Eight more years later, Simpson was convicted of using a deadly weapon to commit kidnapping, burglary, and armed robbery. He admitted trying to steal some of his former belongings, forfeited during his bankruptcy. Simpson served around nine years of his controversially high sentence of thirty-three years. Many speculated over the reasons his sentence was materially higher than those of his two co-conspirators.

Many also became besotted with the Kardashian family. Robert Kardashian, one of the defence team, was O.J.'s college friend. Kris Jenner, Robert's ex-wife, was Nicole's best friend. Kris was married to former Olympic gold medallist Caitlyn Jenner, born William Bruce Jenner, a successful decathlete and now transgender woman. Before the trial, the Kardashian family wasn't in the public eye. Robert died from cancer in 2003, aged fifty-nine, six weeks after marrying his third wife.

30 November 2021

Hubby and I have swapped advent calendars. For the second consecutive year, he's bought me a beauty calendar, the contents of which would cost about four times the calendar price, if bought separately. I'm still using some of last year's amazing contents.

I bought him a wooden refillable one in which I intended to put chocolate brownies, as he had requested. I couldn't find any individually wrapped ones, small enough to fit behind each door and with long enough shelf lives.

After telling him I had been unsuccessful in my mission, despite spending hours looking, he told me he'd sent me a link to one ages ago to save me hunting. I found that message dated 5 September, without any recollection of it, despite it being the same date as another message I remember reading.

I put the loose decorations round the house, a day earlier than I normally would. What difference does one day make? The

Latvian women's football team may think a huge amount. They lost to our Lionesses by twenty goals to nil in a World Cup qualifying match. They may wish they'd been isolating at home.

DECEMBER 2021

1 December 2021

Advent Day

Hubby opened his chocolates, paying little attention to my goo, as he called it.

I went for my biannual health check and sailed through all the initial tests. Apparently I am in the top ten percent of my demographic. Then I met the Doctor who asked me if there was anything concerning me. I told him that the questionnaire I had completed before arriving, churned an automated report that said I should "sort out my depression." I told the Doctor I didn't think I was depressed, although reading that could have tipped me over. He was very apologetic and after a few more questions, concluded the same as me.

He also said I should have another conversation with my GP about HRT. Tell me something I don't know, I thought. I regretted that thought when he told me I had a lump in my right breast.

People say patients don't remember the blur of getting bad news. I remember panicking. Everyone will say breasts, a lot. That word makes me cringe as much as people saying moist does. As for moist breasts. Ewww! I may just be beginning to understand why some people are less freaked out by the C word; the one that isn't Christmas, and doesn't require chemo.

He asked me if the lump was new. It felt tender as I pressed, but I couldn't distinguish it from the lump that is my right bosom. He told me that the lump isn't also present on my left side. The lack of symmetry turned him into a keyboard warrior, typing an urgent referral to see an oncologist, while also suggesting I shouldn't worry!

I went to the toilet for the third time while at the hospital and noticed a sign above the sink about self-examination. Why hadn't I seen that before?

When I got home, I tried booking a consultation. The earliest slot of 9 December 2021 had been taken by the time we'd finished the booking process, and the next available slot is a week after that.

While I'd been on the phone, a colleague emailed my boss and me inviting us to discuss a report she needs to write. Our three diaries won't accommodate this until 21 December 2021.

"That's not soon enough," responded my boss.

I know the feeling. Thankfully my health insurer sent me the names of other oncologists to try. The first hospital I tried hadn't answered the phone after five minutes, so I hung up. I dialled its main competitor and have an appointment to see a breast (yuk) consultant in three days, on Saturday. I was going to make mince pies for the neighbours on Saturday!

2 December 2021

Today's advent goo is hair conditioner. I told Hubby who said he thought my hair looked full-bodied.

"I've not used it yet."

I'm finding it hard to concentrate so am thankful for consecutive remote meetings to keep me focussed on work. I ignore questions in emails that politely ask after me before asking the real reason for the communication. My responses deal with the work-related matters and then wish the reader an enjoyable weekend.

"Glad you're ok," everyone replies, leaving me wondering where I wrote that, but thankful people don't pry further. I simultaneously want to tell everyone I know, and also not tell anyone other than Mr M. I want to feel virtual hugs and love. But I also want to avoid sentiments that seem forced out of obligation, rather than any real empathy.

All I really want is to know if the lump is harmful or not. And I want to know now. And if it is harmful, I want it fixed. Now.

3 December 2021

I couldn't sleep despite trying all mindfulness and other techniques that have worked in the past. I worked from 01:00 until 04:03, hoping I may be able to get some sleep later. Mr M stirred as I delicately climbed back into bed. I started to cry and told him I was scared. Really scared.

He told me what I know I should be thinking. I also think only a robot would stay pragmatic. I have a lump in my right boob. It shouldn't be there. Since knowing, it's seemed painful and tender. I keep checking myself. That's probably a bit late now, and the lump is still there. Is it bigger? I struggled to feel it on Wednesday and now it seems enormous. Hopefully it's just my bosom.

Mr M went to play golf and I managed to sleep until 11:30. I can't stop shaking. It's involuntary. I don't want to shake. I don't want to be scared. I don't want the negative thoughts in my head. Why does my brain let them in when I tell it not to?

Hubby's had his booster. I was told when booking my check-up that I mustn't have had any vaccines in the previous four weeks. Apparently vaccines can affect various tests and their results. So I'm waiting to book my booster until the consultant tells me I can.

Covid can do one. Cancer can do one. And if anyone moans about Christmas being all around us, the thought of which is just about bringing some much needed cheer, they can do one too.

I feel around one hundred. It may take more than the face cleanser that was behind today's advent door to refresh my worry wrinkles.

4 December 2021

Perhaps not surprisingly, I didn't fall asleep before 02:00 again. I wasn't about to get up and work on a Saturday morning. So I just lay there, trying not to disturb SB, breathing comfortingly beside me, blissfully and thankfully unaware of the negativity swimming amongst my brain cells.

I was thinking of all the weekends away we have planned that a shielding chemo patient would have to avoid.

I was wondering when to tell people. Would I tell them before Christmas? It seems unnecessary to ruin it for more than us two, especially after last year. Would I wait until after Dad's eightieth on 19 January 2022? Would I need to excuse myself somehow from his celebrations if any treatment started promptly and I couldn't attend?

We'd miss going to Bath in February for Hubby's birthday, when he's been looking forward to seeing a rugby match there for so long. My own birthday plans would presumably be canned too. There'd be no trip to Exeter with friends, stopping in a lovely hotel followed by a few days in Cornwall for Mr M and me. I'd have to tell our friends in Cornwall we weren't visiting, again, although for a different C this time.

I might just have finished any treatment and be able to join my sister and her fiancé at the hotel we have booked for us four in July. Perhaps I could wear a strapless dress if I've had it removed. I've not been able to wear them since I was about eighteen, so that would at least make a change. I wonder if I could rock the turban look. I've already been looking and seen some that look awesome. Or at least they look awesome on the perfectly chiselled models that adorn them.

Being ill is so inconvenient. Health really is precious and not to be taken for granted. And I might not be ill at all. I don't feel it, other than sick with worry. But if anyone in our family should get it, better that it be me. I'm probably the fittest of the adults, don't have children and have private health care. I'll be fine. Won't I?

Combative thoughts rise and fall like an amusement park

roller coaster. Except it's not amusing. I'm petrified and no one else will ever feel my fear. Even those that are told the same news, or worse, will not feel my fear. We all react differently. We are all unique and our feelings are unique too. Can there be anything more patronising than someone telling you they understand how you feel? They can't. They are different.

It's ironic that all the other health check tests show I am in the top ten percent of my demographic apart from slightly raised cholesterol. That could be peri-menopausal related and isn't cause for undue concern. But I might bloody well have cancer!

Eventually, I remembered some pillow spray a friend sent me last year. It smells like an old sock draw that's been empty and unopened for thirty years, yet it has always helped me sleep before, and it worked again. Genius. Thank you my friend.

Hubby woke me at 09:00 bringing me a cup of tea.

I danced round the bedroom, delighted with today's advent lip balm. Last year's tube is nearly empty so today's gift could hardly have been timed better. Of all the Cs that surround me right now, chapped lips won't be one.

While en route to the hospital to see the oncologist, we picked up the pre-ordered lamb from the butcher. The fire crew's Santa sleigh was parked outside. The friendly butcher, as if there is any other kind, asked me to do my best David Bailey impression of him with one of the firemen who was dressed as Santa. I did so and then dropped a note in the collection bucket.

I always donate to the fire crew at this time of year. They choose to put their lives at risk to save others. It seems even more poignant to donate given my health concerns and the potential threats, through no choice of mine.

Mr M's not allowed into the hospital. He drops me at the door with a parting instruction that I shouldn't go and sit in the sleigh parked on the front lawn! He knows me so well.

While still in the vestibule, I am politely asked to swap my own mask for a hospital-issue one, after which I proceed to reception. The receptionist tells me the oncologist is lovely, and

I will like her. Obviously, I'd rather not have to meet her. But I take comfort from the empathy, and recognition of my potential issue.

I've always hated being ignored, whether it was boyfriends not returning messages, or people ignoring obvious signs of distress instead of asking if they can help me. In what is a very conflicting combination, I've hated being ignored as much as I despise asking for help. When I don't ask for required assistance, I get frustrated when others don't offer it. I get annoyed because I know I would be quicker to offer help than I am to get to the wine fridge on Wednesdays. Mum told me to treat others as I would wish to be treated. I never knew then it would often be unreciprocated.

I've given Hubby a list of things to do in town including collecting my shoes from the mender. He may as well make use of the time as it's pointless driving all the way home again, as he'd have to return almost immediately to collect me.

I'm called for my consultation right on time and follow a lady with a velvety smooth voice into a room. I'm offered a seat by Miss Kaushik who asks why I am there to see her. I'm initially taken aback as I had assumed she would know. Why do I have to repeat it? But then, it may just be part of the usual checks to make sure I'm given the right examination, although I think I'd know if she wasn't looking at the correct part of my anatomy.

She's polite, yet swift. She's kind without being obsequious. After a swift examination of both, she's confident that there's nothing to worry about. She thinks the left, larger and fattier bosom is merely disguising the same lumps which are more apparent in my right one. She orders an ultra-sound to confirm her suspicion. The word suspicion sounds more nocuous than it should.

I feel like I could float and immediately want to message Hubby while I wait for the scan. I haven't got a mobile phone signal. I hope he's alright.

I'm escorted to another waiting area and sit opposite a couple. Both wear wedding rings so I assume they are married, to each other. He has the same brand and colour of trainers as me. I'm not normally observant but his left foot incessantly twitches and caught my lowered eyes. No one wants to make eye contact here. So we stare at people's feet.

I didn't feel any less feminine wearing unisex footwear. But it got me thinking whether I may do so if Miss Kaushik was wrong and I needed a mastectomy. What if she'd only been pacifying me? What if the scan found a malignant tumour? Would my husband see me differently? There'd certainly be a lot less of me. It's not a recommended diet plan.

The lady's been beckoned and I let my eyes rise to read whatever I see. There are posters with names and titles on them. I don't recognise any of the hospital workers. Maybe the posters should have them pictured in masks. A TV screen tells patients not to have any vaccines in the four weeks prior to coming for tests and scans, as the results can be affected. It's a bit late to tell us now.

Hospital workers go about their business. One stops, looks left, and then does a complete about turn and returns from where she came. I wonder if she forgot what it was she was going somewhere to do, as happens to me more and more frequently. Perhaps she'll be back in a few minutes when she's remembered.

I'm called to another small waiting area after being offered a dressing gown.

"Do you have anything in Prada or Dior?" I quip, finding it difficult to mask my simultaneous jollity and nervousness.

"Nothing in a Prada or Dior here, me duck," responds Charlotte, using local terminology that I'd only ever heard said near a pond before living here.

The lady walks down the corridor past me back towards reception. She still has her gown on. I start to wonder if, and hope that, her diagnosis is what she would want it to be. Charlotte calls me into another room.

A gentleman greets me and without another breath he asks me to lie on the bed. He has a required efficiency for those working to fifteen-minute slots and already behind schedule.

I can't see anything other than his assistant in front of me, but sense something massaging me. I have visions of pregnant women being shown a heartbeat, a symbol of a new life, on a screen. I hope the radiologist isn't seeing anything growing in me.

"Did you feel the lump before the Doctor did?"

"To be honest, I couldn't distinguish anything different until he told me, and now it seems like it's more tender than before."

"Ah, well there's a cyst here. Nothing to worry about. I'll just drain it now for you. Say ouch when you feel the scratch."

I don't have time to object or say ouch.

"You didn't say ouch!"

"It didn't hurt! Why would I say ouch? I honestly didn't feel a thing. I've pierced my own belly button so you'll have to try harder than that."

"Press here!"

I start to move my left arm to apply pressure where directed.

"Not you. Charlotte, pressure, here, please!"

Well now I feel like a right tit.

And I feel sorry I ever thought I'd be pleased to get rid of it.

So after around two hours, an empathetic receptionist, a highly qualified consultant, numerous waiting rooms with sanitised chairs, a comfy gown, a bosom massage with some goo that probably cost more than all my advent calendar contents, and a seven inch needle, I am ready to go home.

As soon as I am outside, I ring Hubby to tell him the news we wanted. I'm not sure which of us is happier.

When we get home, we celebrate listening to music and having a few drinks. I drink less than may have been expected in these circumstances, having been told by the oncologist that alcohol consumption increases cancer risks.

"I like this song by *Jack Wolfskin*," I tell Hubby.

"You mean, *Jackson Brown*."

I'm back!

5 December 2021

I slept. I didn't lie awake wondering how I'd get through Christmas without telling family I was ill. I didn't feel frustrated I may have to shield and miss Dad's birthday celebrations while I started treatment. I wasn't sad we wouldn't be able to go to friends' in January or host others at the end of that month, or go on the various other trips we'd planned.

Hubby also slept, until noon. He was exhausted after a stressful few days, not that he had shown he felt stressed. It's exhausting hiding emotions to protect others. He also had his booster on Friday and it doesn't seem to have mixed well with last night's celebrations.

Instead of walking or going to see the Tigers beat Harlequins, we stayed in and watched the game on TV. I made thirty-two orange pastry mince pies and took some round to each of the neighbours.

6 December 2021

I don't have cancer!

7 December 2021

Is it only Tuesday?

8 December 2021

It's a year since Margaret Keenan, then ninety, travelled to the University Hospital, Coventry and became the first person to receive the vaccine. Four hundred and thirty-four billion worldwide have had their first, almost fifty-seven percent of the world's population. England's ninety percent rate brings up that average whereas some low-income countries have only vaccinated around six percent of their residents. Over eight-two percent of England have had two! It continues to be an absolutely remarkable roll-out. Government has set targets, and thanks to so many, they've been achieved.

It doesn't stop me being angry that politicians gathered at the Prime Minister's home last year, partying, in breach of restrictions. While families grieved bereavements, and the sick lay dying on their own, politicians joked and laughed, flouting their own rules.

Hubby said the police are only investigating breaches as they happen. Why aren't they also investigating alleged past infringements? The police don't only investigate murders and other crimes where they catch the perpetrator in the act.

How can our Prime Minister expect the country to adhere to any future restrictions? I only hope this doesn't dissuade him from imposing them if that is what's required.

18:00

He's announced increased restrictions from Monday. We must work from home if we can, and wear masks in more places. Certain venues and events will also need to see a Covid pass or vaccine passport.

The medical advisors are doing their best to explain why these measures are necessary. Research shows more people respond more positively to a request if they understand the underlying rationale. Case numbers of the Omicron variant are doubling every three days and possibly more rapidly. If we don't hinder the spread, our NHS may not cope and excess deaths will increase again. I'd like to think most people understand that, and would want to help avoid it.

But I don't understand why supposedly intelligent people, entrusted to take all necessary steps to keep us safe, were rubbing shoulders a year ago, laughing about doing so, while the country mourned and suffered.

9 December 2021

The usual year-end rush at work is at full throttle, as we scurry to clear desks and hit targets. We're also blessed to have a new recruit to train, which is welcome. Her enthusiasm is contagious and her previous work experiences will benefit us all.

10 December 2021

We've been invited out for a meal for a friend's birthday. Mutual friends who live in the village have offered to drive, as he doesn't drink. The restaurant to which we're going still has a bottle of red that we bought and paid for months ago when it was the last available. The meal sill costs eighty pounds per couple, which may be why many seem to be changing their spending habits and staying at home more.

12 December 2021

I've decorated the living room Christmas tree, twelve days after I had intended.

13 December 2021

Lots of people are finishing on Friday for a break over the festive period, and so the usual last minute requests to "just" do this and that before they are on leave continue. I doubt I'll be able to respond to them all. What's the worst that can happen if I can't?

14 December 2021

I received some feedback today from some psychometric tests I completed during an unsuccessful interview process. It's unusual for potential employers to take this time with unsuccessful candidates, and I'm very grateful. I wasn't given the position as I don't live as near to one of the firm's offices as another candidate who performed as well as me in the tests. Despite increased working flexibility, they have decided they'd prefer someone who may more easily attend an office more regularly.

I'm buoyed by the very positive feedback. I feel like I have, and can add, value. I am pleased to hear the results confirm I clearly have morals and standards by which I stand, even when faced with challenge. The comments give my dented confidence a real boost.

Over twenty-four million have had the booster. Government has set a target of one million per day and to have boosted all adults by the end of this month. My appointment is on 11 January 2022.

I received a text from my Australian godsons' grandmother. Sadly I forgot to sign the cheque I sent her to cover the cost of their gifts. Even more tragically, she didn't notice until she'd arrived at the bank. With her subsequent agreement, I have sent funds electronically.

15 December 2021

There's been over seven hundred and forty-five thousand booster jabs today.

Hubby has hibernated his Facebook account, hoping his mood is boosted by not reading as much negativity. It's been around fifteen months since I stopped using my account, and remains one of my best decisions of 2020 and since.

16 December 2021

There's been over eighty-eight thousand new cases in one day and one hundred and forty-six deaths within twenty-eight days of a positive test.

Last year, when deaths exceeded three figures for the first time, I cried.

17 December 2021

I'm not sure whether the Omicron variant is spreading any more quickly than those who have symptoms of "Oh-my-ffs-let's-get-on". It's been around since early pandemic days, but was limited to pockets of the population, seemingly most common amongst those that resisted vaccines or opposed lockdowns.

Over the last twenty-one months, it's gained momentum, sneaking up, and even impregnating those that had been adamant they would shield until the end of the pandemic.

Its spread will be of as much concern to the vulnerable as the existing Delta and Omicron variants. The vulnerable will be much less susceptible to Oh-my-ffs-LGO, but its spread increases the risk of other variant cases increasing. The vulnerable will need to continue to isolate away from exposure, as our ancestors once hid in shelters during air-raids. Are invisible wars worse and more difficult to overcome? They certainly seem non-negotiable. Virus mutations have the potential to gazump whatever our scientists come up with, slowly sinking our vaccine battleships to ineffectiveness, pending reinforcements that allow us all to resurface.

Mr M and I shall certainly be even more cautious this close to seeing family, especially as I haven't yet had my reinforcing booster. Perhaps I should bring that forward? There's been over ninety-three thousand new cases today.

Increasing numbers and also the recent news of rule-flouting parties, are likely to have contributed to the Conservative Party's defeat in North Shropshire, where it's held a seat for almost two hundred years. The gentleman appointed to investigate those parties, apparently had his own. Some think it's a joke and not a very funny one.

It's also sad to read that two sets of young twins died in a house fire after possible neglect, for which a woman's been arrested. For some, it is not the most wonderful time of the year.

I remember my grandad telling me about a really jolly person with whom he spoke while wating in a surgery once. My grandad asked him how he stayed so cheerful, especially given their location at the time. The man didn't read the news or watch TV. There wasn't any social media then either. He found joy living his life, without the adverse influences that reading and seeing sad news can bring.

I'm elated by the arrival of the wrapping paper carry case I ordered. I won't need to prop wrapping paper tubes in wardrobe corners anymore.

My great aunt is eighty-five today and I'm thrilled she manages to speak to me despite ill health and pain. She's been unwell for months and I hope for better for her in 2022, and certainly by May when Mr M and I are going to visit. My sister and family, and we, have also booked a three-night mini-break to spend with our parents in August 2022, near where she lives, so my sister can meet her for the first time.

Hubby broke my thoughts telling me that Bruce Springsteen has sold his music rights for half a billion dollars. I told him I'd buy some new shoes if I had half a billion.

"You don't need any new shoes!"

18 December 2021

The hair salon is full. The women are all reading magazines. The men are all either saying they've put weight on since having children and have to squeeze into a panto costume later, or are asking the women for present ideas for their partners.

19 December 2021

We ate breakfast out with our two friends that join us at rugby matches, then hosted them at ours to watch the game on TV. It felt much safer than mingling with thousands, even outdoors.

We mooted when another lockdown would commence. Will Dad's lunch on 16 January 2022 be allowed? I couldn't attend my parents' golden wedding anniversary in May due to the rule of six at the time, but remind myself that all that matters is that they are still here.

Emma Radacanu won Sports Personality of the Year, aged nineteen. I'm not sure I had much of a personality when I was that age. I certainly wasn't a Grand Slam winner. The only slamming I did involved tequila. I was pretty good at it.

21 December 2021

Mr Johnson has told us there won't be any more restrictions before Christmas. I'm not sure how many would pay attention to be honest.

Our Chancellor has announced more support for businesses that have been financially impacted by reduced trade as potential customers worry about the virus risks. It sounds like most, if not all, of the funds will be directed at the hospitality sector. I wonder about other sectors, including sport. Some clubs will have seen their income decimated since March 2020, and they must be desperate for additional funds.

Hubby's just managed to buy two tickets for the rugby match between Bath and Leicester Tigers when we go to Bath for a weekend in mid-February to celebrate his birthday. I nearly fell over when he said each ticket cost sixty pounds.

22 December 2021

The number of daily cases has exceeded one hundred thousand for the first time.

We're hosting my folks for Christmas for the first time this year, and they arrive tomorrow. I've made two curries. One is slightly milder for Mum. I've also made some shortbread and will do more mince pies tomorrow after work.

I have been guilty of inwardly criticising parents that cook more than one dish for their children. I have often wondered why people take on so much for their offspring, feeding them what they choose, and driving them to various events and clubs, when their bedrooms packed with items for their amusement, are just a few stairs away. Perhaps my desire to make sure my parents enjoy themselves is similar. I love them dearly, but three nights, not eighteen years, will be quite sufficient.

I can't remember our fridge ever being so full of food!

23 December 2021

They're here and Mum's malapropisms start almost instantly, which reminds Dad of a story from years ago. Mum was working in the local Council's valuation office. She had to visit properties to assess their rateable values. On one occasion, she was going to a house whose owner had just completed an extension.

On arrival, a gentleman answered the door, towering over my petite mum.

"I've come to measure your erection!"

24 December 2021

My folks have come with their own porridge and various other preferred food items, as if we don't have shops in Leicester. Regardless, they eat the same as the rest of us, not least as my attempts at porridge looked worse than my treacle toffee.

It's a good job I'm not working today as it's 10:30 before I have time for a shower. I descend to noises of someone unfamiliar with our kitchen attempting to do something. It's mother, trying to make a coffee. She can't even lift our jug kettle which is too heavy for her.

"Please let me do it, Mum. Just ask me if you need something," I say while thinking it's not been ten minutes since she had a cup of tea!

How can it be lunchtime? How do parents ever make it to work on time? Looking after other people is a full-time job.

Mum offers for the forty-second time to help me make mince pies. I tell her there's no need, and instead, after our meal this evening, she can help lay the Christmas table.

I also make the stuffing before Hubby returns from golf and then get the evening meal ready. I clear up as the family retires to the living room.

Mum enters the kitchen just as I have finished laying the table for tomorrow.

"That looks lovely sweetie-pie!"

Cheers Mum, I think, while suddenly panicking one of us doesn't like tomorrow's planned starter. Mr M has a backup plan to make pâté from the bird's livers. Thankfully I am mistaken. We all like the menu. Why do we allow ourselves to get so stressed? It's not like we won't have enough to eat, like so many underprivileged.

We all take negative tests ahead of tomorrow and now it's gin time.

25 December 2021

Christmas Day

00:01

We stayed up with my folks and opened our presents. The last time I did that was at theirs with my sister when I was around fourteen I think. We vowed never to do it again, although I'm grateful now for the extra time it gives us today.

Hubby bought me a new smart watch with the health apps. I really must do more cardiovascular exercise.

I've no idea how many steps I had done by the time we sat down to eat, but the benefits of all the activity were soon to be negated. The crackers gave such a disproportionately loud bang, I think my heart skipped several beats.

They were considerably smaller than I had expected, but I'd not realised my faux pas until they'd arrived and were fit for my teddy bear. I couldn't be bothered to return them, and they took less room on the already busy table anyway. As an added bonus, they didn't include a useless plastic toy that would have ended up in landfill.

We ate and we talked. We ate some more and talked some more. We didn't watch a film as we usually do, or try to convince our guests to play some games. We just talked until it was time to go to bed. I loved every minute and the six of us being together was more of a gift than I could have wished for.

26 December 2021

It's Boxing Day, so called as it was traditionally a day off for servants who would receive a Christmas box from their masters.

We're all negative, so can meet my sister and family for lunch in Cheshire. Sadly Desmond Tutu's family can't spend time with him anymore. He died today aged ninety. He was a South African Anglican bishop and theologian. He was a human rights activist who also worked against apartheid, for which he won a Nobel Peace Prize and other awards. He was also the first black African to be both Bishop of Johannesburg, a position he held for around a year from 1985, and Archbishop of Cape Town for the following decade. Rest in peace.

I thought the restaurant would be busier but am glad to feel safe from the space around us. After staying home for the majority of the last twenty-one months, we don't want to start 2022 with Covid.

27 December 2021

I woke up with a sore throat and so am glad my test is negative. We will continue with daily tests after being out yesterday, although the restaurant was well spaced and we wore masks and sanitised.

Hubby's playing golf. I have cleared the dining room table, tidied the sofas, and put some washing in. I feel shattered. Holidays are tiring.

I rang my dad's cousin to see how their aunt is doing. It's strange to think I may not be here if my paternal grandad had survived the war. It doesn't stop me being angry and upset when Hitler is mentioned on QI. People laughed at the joke and I know that being offended is pointless. I mustn't discourage the discussions, whatever the form. If we don't continue to have the conversations, those atrocities could recur. They already are in some parts of the world.

Why does it feel like more pioneering people die at this time of year than any other? April Ashley died today aged eighty-six. She was an English model, actress and author, outed as transgender in 1961 by a newspaper. She is one of the first British people known to have had sex reassignment surgery. I can't imagine either how she felt to be able to choose to live as she believed she should have been born, or how she felt when her marriage was annulled on the grounds she was a man. In those days, marriage between two men was void. I wonder if she found it painful to have it annulled when her husband knew her history when they wed, or whether she was grateful it was deemed void.

28 December 2021

I'm negative again but feel tired after all the excitement. I also feel sad for England's male cricket team. They were all out for sixty-eight runs and beaten by an innings and fourteen runs. The Australian team has an unassailable three-nil lead in a five test series. Sadly, the locals haven't been tested that much.

I hope it wasn't a miserable Christmas for our team. Living out of hotels can be lonely, and far from as enjoyable as the decadent sound of being waited on suggests. In addition to being away from home comforts, the team's liberties have been further restricted by the pandemic, on top of which, many of their own fans won't help fill the stadiums. Many would feel defeated by the mental challenge presented by the combination of so many adverse factors. Shouldn't we give the team a rest? We could give them a break from the various other formats of the game that mean they're not able to spend time rehearsing the longer game. Our future generations won't be interested in test cricket if we can't compete.

29 December 2021

Booster day

Another negative test although how I will work for a day while this tired is beyond me. At least I won't get many emails, calls or queries. They'll probably be a record low. Unlike our daily cases, which has exceeded one hundred and eighty thousand, a record high. Hospitalisations are far from their peak, although they are the highest since 1 March 2021 with almost ten and a half thousand, up forty-eight percent from last week. It'll be a miracle if we avoid it, despite hardly going anywhere.

Admittedly, some of the hospitalisations are people admitted for something else. It's also more difficult to discharge patients at this time of year. What is worrying is that those who are seriously unwell from the recent variant are rising, although trends suggest infection levels in our capital may have peaked. I'll be glad to be boosted having brought my appointment forward.

11:15

The service was extremely efficient. I suppose nowhere wants people hanging around for longer than necessary. Hubby's kindly driven me, although the requirement to wait for fifteen minutes has been dropped anyway. As I climb back in his car, I ask him if I should be concerned that the seat on which I sat to be vaccinated wasn't sanitised between patients, as done at the other station. The medic's mask had slipped a couple of times too. The sanitiser bottle I received for Christmas that attaches to my belt loop has certainly been useful; it would be ironic if I caught it from the booster centre.

17:00

I've survived a working day and feel like I would if I was coming down with flu, which seems quite common after a booster.

21:00

I'm so cold, I'm going to bed.

30 December 2021

I feel like a zombie after waking every two hours and am aching all over. I'm still testing negative so it looks like our Boxing Day lunch was lurgy free.

I may as well stop testing now as we're not going anywhere anyway. Ghislaine Maxwell could face the same fate after being found guilty on five out of six charges, including the most serious. She's expected to appeal the conviction for her involvement in Epstein's sexual abuse of teenage girls. Prosecutors said she "preyed on vulnerable young girls, manipulated them and served them up to be sexually abused." She is expected to receive a significant prison term, which could last her remaining years alive.

Hubby's roasting beside me in the study as I've got the portable heater on in a vain attempt to warm my bones. Even a bath after work didn't completely take away the chill. Is this how it feels to sleep outdoors in winter? I've not been this cold when ski-ing, although the correct clothing will have helped. Perhaps I should put my ski gear on.

I managed to stay up until 22:00.

31 December 2021

I've got razor blades in my throat, ache all over including my eye lids and am shivering. On top of which, after another poor night's sleep, I'm not fit to concentrate today. It serves me right for recently feeling very smug that I would manage the entire calendar year without any sick leave, and now have had two days in just over a month.

My lateral flow test is positive. The PCR booking system is taking me round in frustrating circles. I had thought it would be easy although it may just be me. Hubby's managed to book a PCR appointment for me, although it seems likely it will also be positive. I had mistakenly thought I was suffering from the effects of the booster.

I've checked, and the booster can't give a false positive result. The lines on the tests have never been stronger than today. Great. I hope the rest of our family stay negative. Hubby and I have been cautious, even more so in the days before seeing family over the festive period.

We've put a note on the door to alert people to my positive status. We could have gone for the smutty option about the sanitised knocker and flap, but decided this wasn't any time to be flippant.

At least we will still receive post and food deliveries. In 1665, the Lord Mayor of London's regulations stated, "That every house visited [by the plague] be marked with a red cross of a foot long in the middle of the door, evident to be seen." Occupants wrote above the cross "Lord, have mercy upon us."

It looks like a beautiful day, a change from the recent murkiness, so typical of this time of year. But a dark shadow hangs over our capital, with the report of another teenage homicide. That's a record of thirty this year, two more than the previous record eighteen years ago. There's been twenty-seven stabbings, two shootings and one case of suspected arson. The 2008 statistic was never a target to be exceeded! Whatever the circumstances, thirty young lives have been lost prematurely this year due to violent crime. Thirty too many. Why are the numbers amongst teenagers going up when violent crime is generally declining?

In addition, forty teenagers in London have been charged with murder this year. Where is our society going wrong? Violence is raging like the wildfires currently engulfing Colorado, destroying hundreds of buildings, killing, and injuring in their wake. Why do so many of our young carry lethal weapons?

Some will blame Government, the schools, social media, or violent computer games. I didn't have the latter two as a child and the first two didn't need to tell me right from wrong. But what about children who aren't taught right from wrong at home for whatever reason? Who picks up the gap? Is it right to assume we're born knowing right from wrong when other behaviours are learned? The Ten Commandments include thou shalt not kill. Are they still taught in schools?

What would the R rate be for a teenager carrying a lethal weapon. How many may be injured or killed? I can't remember when I last read what our virus R rate was. After checking, I struggle to believe it's still teetering around only one in all areas. There were almost one hundred and ninety thousand cases on Friday and over two hundred and three deaths reported. I remember crying the first time the death rate exceeded three figures in a day.

Is part of the current increase because we have become desensitised to statistics that had us reeling a year or more ago, before Professors Chris Whitty and Van-Tam became household names? They have both been knighted in the New Year Honours List 2022, in recognition of their achievements and service. Both men regularly brief the nation from Downing Street and will have "Sir" before their names. Sir Whitty is the Chief Medical Officer for England and chief medical advisor to the government. As well as fronting briefings and TV campaigns, he's a practising NHS consultant at London hospitals, and represents the UK on the executive board of the World Health Organisation. To think he was subject to abuse earlier in the year, as he walked our streets, and needed police intervention. Professor Van-Tam has been the Deputy Chief Medical Officer for England since 2017, and captured our imaginations with his metaphors.

Dr Jenny Harries, Chief Executive of the UK Health Security Agency, and Dr June Raine, head of the vaccine regulator MHRA, are both made Dames.

Government's Chief Scientific Advisor, Professor Sir Patrick Vallance was knighted in the 2019 List and has been elevated to the same rank as Sir Whitty, that of Knight Commander of the Order of the Bath. George I founded the order of chivalry on 18 May 1725. The elaborate medieval ceremony included bathing, a symbol of purification, and so the individuals became known as Knights of the Bath.

The Chief Medical Officers for Wales and Scotland, Frank Atherton and Professor Gregor Smith respectively, are also knighted, and the lady who led England's vaccination deployment, Emily Lawson, becomes a dame.

A friend to whom I recently sent some honey when she was ill, has sent me a gift of ten mini bath gels. She thought I may need cheering up from my enforced isolation. It works, as does watching the usual year-end entertainment. I never knew what a Hootenanny was before! It turns out, I feel brighter just saying it out loud. The host introduces his next singer and we both thought he said she'd be singing a Queen song. He'd said Cream.

Hubby quizzically asks me who was in Cream. He has to tell me it was Eric Clapton, although it would have made more sense if I hadn't misheard and thought he'd said Eric Chaplain. As midnight approaches, Hubby toasts good riddance to 2021.

I ask him what was so bad about it, the obvious aside. Unlike in 2020, we didn't lose close family and friends and we saw friends and family at last. We were mostly healthy. We had food on the table and a roof over our heads. We stayed in employment and Hubby continued to get positive feedback and requests for more varied work. Yes, we cried. We also laughed a lot. Life has laughter everywhere, even if it's hard to bring yourself to smile. And we know that even when we don't feel like smiling, we will again. Every sentiment passes with time. It's also the warmest New Year's Eve in the UK on record, which is good for keeping the heating bills down if nothing else.

I think he rethinks his assessment, and we wish for a healthy 2022.

JANUARY 2022

1 January 2022

Happy New Year. It's official. The PCR result confirms I have Covid. It's not cancer. Hopefully it won't kill me. And Mr M has said I can do nothing after yesterday's breathless episodes, so that's another positive result. I am too breathless to start the year with the number of steps I managed almost a year ago, so I'll just take it one step at a time and be pleased I can take each one.

Mum messaged me to say her and Dad are going out for lunch, while I isolate at home. No doubt she meant there'd be no point me ringing to wish them happy New Year while they're out. I'm sure she didn't mean to provoke jealously of their liberty, while we're legally bound to stay at home.

We've just heard a friend's Mum died last night. I'm instantly very thankful mine can go for lunch.

Our isolation will prevent us seeing friends on 8 January 2022, one of whom is waiting for us to return a hip flask he left here pre-pandemic. I'm sure the contents have been evaporating.

2 January 2022

Hubby is positive. At least two of his golf mates are also positive, together with the daughter of a couple we know, and her partner, and also the son of another friend, for the second time. None of these cases are connected that we know of. Most aren't too unwell, although tiredness seems common to us all.

I can breathe though my nose and also fit in my wedding dress again. Who loses weight over Christmas? Hubby and I have finally had a New Year hug. It could be worse.

We'll be able to go out soon enough, without the fears that those who are vulnerable may feel. For those families, it may be more worrying to send their children to school, risking them returning with the virus, than to keep them at home. For those families, it may still be advisable to stay indoors, while the rest of us may feel freedom has returned.

I feel blessed.

3 January 2022

I feel more out of breath than yesterday. Hubby's keeping busy as he can't play golf. Typically, it's another beautiful day. I miss things more when I am told I can't do them, even if self-imposed. When I've tried to abstain from anything in the past, I've continually thought about whatever it is I am prohibited from having. I find it easier to succeed with abstention if I harbour a thought that I will allow myself to concede if I really want to. I live in the twenty-first century after all, not the prohibition.

It's different of course, at the moment. It's illegal to go out while positive. I'd love to go out for a walk today. I would love to try the functionality on my new watch. The sky is blue. The air is fresh and crisp and still, concealing the threat that invisibly surrounds us all. I know some who would break the law. I will wait. We stayed indoors for longer periods in 2020 so can cope again.

I'm back at work tomorrow so regardless of the restrictions to which we must adhere, I shall enjoy the last day of my leave. I won't get it back. I won't get any of my days back. I can, at least partially, control the script of my future days. I may not be able to go out for walks right now, but I'm determined to write thousands of great steps, every day.

What will you do?

Acknowledgements

This book wouldn't have started without my sister-in-law and her husband, who bought me the most beautiful journal as a gift, in which I started to write.

Thanks to the agents that assured me this narrative merited a place in anyone's library.

I'll be eternally grateful to those from whom I received encouragement when they read my updates: Chez-la and Anna B; Keegs; LS; Sis; Mum; Kate C-J; Wendy & Gerry and your friends for their independent view.

I wouldn't have finished it without my husband suggesting I publish it as I am 'funnier in writing than in real life.' Thanks SB, I think, and I know I'm indebted for your patience and love.

Thanks to all the friends, family, colleagues, tutors, mentors, and others who've helped me when I was sailing what felt to me like the roughest waters. Some of you may recall some of the events in this book, and all of you have helped me keep being me. I'm pleased it will make sure I never forget how much all your friendships and guidance continue to mean to me.

Final thanks is to you, the reader. I hope it brings you at least some of the help and joy that writing it brought to me.

If you enjoyed it, please share recommendations and compliments. If you didn't, please choose kind.

Lord, keep us safe this night
Secure from all our fears
May angels guard us while we sleep
'Til morning light appears

Thank you.

About The Author

Annabelle Z Morris

was born in her bedroom in Blackburn. She moved to Leicester-shire almost thirty years ago, where she lives with her husband. She is a chartered accountant, rugby and cricket fan, and this is her first book.

Praise For Author

Annabelle's musings take us through the second year of the pandemic. Peppered with gentle life philosophies learnt over the decades, this will have you laughing and crying, as her experiences resonate with your own. This book is a hug to everyone who has got this far.

'You're funnier in writing than in person.'

- MR M

Printed in Great Britain
by Amazon

83R00129